The Ultimate H

The Ultimate Power

Dave Grant

Fleming H. Revell Company
Old Tappan, New Jersey

Library of Congress Cataloging in Publication Data

Grant, Dave.
   The ultimate power.

   Bibliography: p.
   1. Conduct of life.   2. Success.   3. Love.   I. Title.
BJ1581.2.G674   1983   158'.1   82-22964
ISBN 0-8007-1337-0

This book is dedicated to all
The Great Lovers at my house:
Simone
Brenda
Julene
Celeste
Kevin

Contents

Preface

The material for this book has been taken primarily from the content of a seminar, "The Maximum Performer," that I have been teaching for the past ten years. During those ten years I have presented more than a thousand seminars to over a hundred thousand participants from all walks of life.

In the seminars the Self-Esteem Exercise and Values Inventory included in this book were given to each participant.

Wanting to get a focus on the general response of the participants, we decided to do a computer analysis. We collected exercises from respondents representing the fields of sales, management, education, the professions, and religion.

The data was analyzed by a PDP 11/34 computer using selected programs from the BMDP-77 "package" of statistical programs.

Here are some of the results of that data: Of the combined five groups, 11.9 percent were considered to have *low* self-esteem; 63.8 percent, average self-esteem; and 24.3 percent, *high* self-esteem. The group with the highest self-esteem was from sales, followed by management, religion, education, and the professions.

In regards to motivation, 29.14 percent listed love as the main motivator in their life and 70.86 percent listed fear.

Success was defined in terms of "doing something" by 56.06 percent, and 43.94 percent defined success in terms of "being somebody."

To the question, "What do you want most out of life?" the answer given most frequently was "a good relationship." The second most frequent answer was "happiness."

9

The impact of love and/or fear or who we *are* and what we *do* is what this book is all about. In reading it you will receive some tools and insights for establishing richer, more rewarding relationships.

Sincerely,

Dave Grant

Unit I

How Love Overcomes the Power of Fear

- Only Love Can Beat the System's Standard

- What Do You Have to Lose?

- How to *Really* Be Somebody

- The Things We Do for Love

1

Only Love Can Beat the System's Standard

If bumper stickers reveal the truths and philosophies of our culture, one would be inclined to believe that all of us think we are—or would like to be—great lovers. And, if we can believe what we are told, everything from drinking milk to being a cowboy will help us fulfill this ambition.

But from what Madison Avenue and the mass media have been telling us, there's more to being a great lover than one would first believe. Great lovers are also great dressers, great dancers, great shoppers. They go to the right stores, drink the right wines, drive the right cars. They use the right hair sprays, toothpastes, deodorants. They are happy, beautiful people who succeed on the job, in the marketplace, and in their bedrooms. They always come in first.

There has been a commercial on television advertising an oil product (Number 1, of course!). As the driver gets into his race car and pulls away, he leaves us with this little dig: "Nobody ever remembers who came in second place." And we all want to be remembered, don't we? What have we been told we have to do to be remembered? Why, nothing—except be Number 1 in whatever we *do*. Or be a "10" in how we *look*. Or, have a 4.0 grade point average in what we *know*.

Why have we been deluged with this not always subtle message? It's because all of us share three basic human desires: Everyone wants to be happy, successful, and loved. Knowing this, society inundates us with all kinds of conflicting ideas. We've been told:

- How to win through intimidation.
- How to get and use power over people.
- How to take care of "number one."
- How to be $ucce$$ful.
- How to find fulfillment by pulling our own strings.

One group says "belief is nothing," but another group says that the secret to life is meditation. Another voice tells us the answer is "Management by Objectives." We don't know whether to live in the now or to lay out goals and plans for the rest of our lives.

We've been inspired, threatened, exhorted, and cajoled by an intangible, obscure anonymity; and not knowing what name to give it, we call it *they. They* plague us with guilt and shame if we're not winners—by *their* standards. *They* determine which fashions are "in" and which are "out." *They* hold us responsible if our kids don't make the team or fail to show up on the Dean's List. Just where did *they* come from anyway? How did their system develop? Who gave them the right to run our lives? *We did!* We did, because we wanted to be remembered. We wanted to be somebody.

Is there an explanation for this obsession to be somebody? I believe there is from both personal observation and historical precedent. From early childhood it is obvious we have a cosmic ache for specialness. One has only to listen to the complaints of young siblings to understand our desperate need to be valuable and unique and important:

"You gave him more juice!"

"Here's a little more, then."

"Now *she's* got more than me!"

And so it goes. Rarely do we hear a child say, "That's not fair! You gave him *less* than me!" We can all remember the concern we had that we get our share; that no one got more. We fought for equality (and still do) in order to keep somebody else from getting ahead. The desire for "more" or "better" is seldom overcome. We all want to be held in high esteem, to be considered

most worthy and to be the best loved. The Smothers Brothers
even made a national joke out of "Mom always liked you best."
Sibling rivalry simply expresses the tragic hold the system has on
all of us: We must *prove* that we are significant, and to be significant we must be the *best* or Number 1!

Since Creation, history has been replete with man's struggle
for significance. In his book *The Greatest Miracle in the World,*
Og Mandino proposes a modern historical hypothesis as to
what may have dealt a near fatal blow to our self-worth. It may
have begun when Copernicus proved that the earth is not the
center of the universe, that our planet is really just a tiny
speck moving through space. Learning that we are insignificant
compared to the vastness of the universe is a jolt to our
specialness.

Mandino further suggests that two other men also influenced
our view of ourselves. First, Darwin proposed that we were not
special creations of God, but had simply evolved from the animal
kingdom. Our animal instincts were given license. If we were just
animals, why shouldn't we breed like animals and kill for the survival of the fittest like all the other animals? Then Freud told us
that we were unable to control many of our actions because of
childhood experiences buried deep within our subconscious
minds. There was only just so much for which we could be held
responsible. It became easy—even fashionable—to blame our
environment or our parents for our behavior. We just "couldn't
help it."

As a result of these influences, Mandino drew this conclusion:

> If we are not Godlike people, if we do not live in the center of
> God's world, if we are really only animals, and if we cannot con-
> trol and explain many of our actions, then we are not of any
> more consequence than the weeds in our garden. If we are not, in
> truth, very much of anything, then how can we be proud of our-
> selves? And if we are not proud of what we are, how can we like
> ourselves? And if we don't like ourselves, who wants to live with
> that sort of person?

In spite of the onslaught, most people have maintained a spark that keeps them going. We persist in trying to make it in the system without realizing that the system has virtually made it impossible for us to succeed, either personally or professionally—by their standard. To get a little insight into how the system perpetuates itself, let's consider what happens in Los Angeles County where there are approximately one million students in elementary school through college.

On any campus, who are the somebodies? They are
the Good Lookers
the Brains
the Achievers

What percentage of the entire one million students do all these categories represent? Probably 5 percent, but let's be generous and say 10 percent. That means our school system helps to perpetuate society's conditions for being somebody—and ends up producing 900,000 *nobodies!* And then people wonder why young people do all the crazy things they do. They just want to be somebody, but they live in a society that makes it virtually impossible—by their standards.

When we all started out we were going to be somebody; maybe even *better* than anyone else. We were going to prove to everybody just how good and important we were. And how many people worked hard, day and night, climbing the ladder to the top, only to discover it was leaning against the wrong wall.

Most people will never make it to the top—by the system's standard. Most people will never be Number 1—by the system's standard. Most people will never be winners—by the system's standard. The message has come through loud and clear that if you don't come in first, you're not only a loser, you're a bad guy. We all know that bad guys don't *deserve* to be loved.

Yet we persist with the system. And the deeper we get into the system, the more we lose—by the system's standards. And the more we experience losing, the more frightened we become.

Out of fear comes anger. In anger, we lash out, trying to find someone or something to blame because we feel threatened and manipulated and hurt. But the system says we can't give up. We can't be quitters. We must try harder, especially if we are only Number 2. And the harder we try, the sooner we die.

We need to stop and think of what we've been doing and the effect it has had on our lives and on the lives of those we say we love. All along we've been saying we were doing it for them, but too often the payoff has been broken, bitter relationships, alienated children, and an emptiness inside that won't go away.

Regaining Control of Our Lives

Are we locked into the system, or is there something we can do about it? Can we regain control of our lives and still attain those basic desires of happiness, success, and love? I think it is obvious that we are faced with a choice: either we stick with the system or we abandon it.

If we stick with the system, we must keep on competing, keep on blaming ourselves for "failing," try harder, work longer hours. We must keep blaming our parents, or our spouses, or our circumstances, or "luck," for holding us back and continue to pursue the elusive security of being better looking, or smarter, or more effective in what we do. And in the end we lose touch with reality, our values, and those loving relationships that make life meaningful.

If we abandon the system, we must admit that we bought into something that can't work and stop blaming, rationalizing, scapegoating, comparing, and competing. We must realize that we did fail to meet the system's standard—and it's okay! Then we can replace the system with something else. Something that works for *anybody*.

Psychologist Alfred Adler stated that "all human failure is the result of a lack of love." If Adler is correct, and I believe he is, we cannot succeed in life unless we stop struggling to be somebody and begin to love. Nearly twenty centuries ago an intense and wise old man who lived in Asia Minor did just that. His name was

John, and he had once bought into the system of which we have been speaking.

Somewhere along the line, John came to realize that the answers to all of his desires lay in the path of love, and he wrote, "There is no fear in love. But perfect love drives out fear. . . ."[1] The power of love to conquer fear is what this book is all about.

It's true that the term *great lover* has a double meaning. More often than not, when people are referred to as great lovers, they are in reality just the opposite. Frequently they are takers—using other people for their own gratification.

Loving Great Equals Living Great

We don't have to shy away from the term *great lover* just because its meaning has been distorted. A truly great lover is one who loves. To love great is to live great. We cannot live any better than we love. Therefore, love is the key to successful living.

There is a strong correlation between love and success as well as between fear and failure. We do not love because of fear; fear leads to failure in performance, in gaining happiness, and in building successful relationships. If we fail to understand how fear and love affect our lives and motivate us, we will continue to buy into the system.

I have often thought that some schools of psychology had a pretty good understanding of this problem but could offer no real solution. On the other hand, I felt that those who practice the Judeo–Christian ethic had the solution but often failed to understand the problem.

One of my hopes is that this book will bridge some of the gap between the psychological and the theological; between the extremes of narcissism and self-condemnation; between the humanist and the religionist; between the secular and the sacred. The humanist hasn't taken seriously the fall of man and his subsequent imperfection. He has been told he can be somebody all

---

1. 1 John 4:18 NIV

by himself, but he suffers from the nagging fear that maybe he can't really save himself.

Too many religious people have been convinced they are nobodies and can do nothing for themselves. They have been convinced they are worms who deserve nothing good and, consequently, use piety as a cover for fear and fatalism and confuse low self-esteem with humility.

This is reality: No one can buy or achieve success, happiness, self-sufficiency, immortality, or love. No one can earn self-worth, and no one has to "deserve" it. Our self-worth is a given. What we've been working so hard to get, we've already got! *A self worth loving!* We each have infinite value, and because of that, our worth cannot be determined in comparison to someone else's. We need not live in despair; our humanity has been redeemed.

I AM AN UNREPEATABLE MIRACLE

Therefore, we need to learn to be good to ourselves, to be compassionate, to be understanding, to be loving. We can stop the fearful, competitive struggle to be somebody. We can be great lovers.

The principles and tools offered here are designed to bring us to the place where we can better utilize our skills to release our God-given resources and *enjoy* them—whether we win or lose. We can pursue the excellence of living with balance and compassion.

There is no limit as to who can be a great lover. I know great lovers who are salespeople, and managers, and home executives, and students, and teachers, and parents, and many others. Anyone who wants to can be a great lover.

The true success of our lives will not be judged by those who admire us for our accomplishments, but by those who attribute their wholeness to our loving them, by those who have seen their true beauty and worth in our eyes. That's the measure of a great lover.

When we realize that we were created special, unrepeatable miracles, destined to be great lovers, the end result will not be conceit, but gratitude.

Step One to Becoming a Great Lover: Make a conscious decision to abandon the system's standard of honoring only superlatives and become a great lover.

Workshop:

1. Let me suggest that before you go on to the next chapter you take a few minutes to take the Self-Esteem Exercise and Values Inventory that is included in the Appendix. This is designed to get you in touch with how you see yourself and some of the things that are important to you. This is a book about healthy motivation, and we need to understand that we are motivated by our values; productive achievement is a consequence and an expression of self-esteem, not its cause. All through the book I will be referring to the answers and responses in these exercises. When you have finished reading the book, you may want to take the exercises again to check for the movement in your life.
2. Are there areas in your life that you would like to be happier and more successful?
3. Do you understand what the "system" is and how you can beat it?
4. Do you fall under either of these extremes?
   (a) I am somebody all by myself.
   (b) I am a nobody and I can therefore do nothing for myself.
5. With positive thoughts only, meditate on the meaning of this statement: **I am an unrepeatable miracle.**

2

What Do You Have to Lose?

Every now and then the newspapers report a situation similar to one that occurred recently in the affluent community of West Palm Beach, Florida. An elderly woman had been going door to door, begging for food. Apparently she didn't get enough nourishment, because she ended up in the hospital, suffering from malnutrition. Because of her age and the seriousness of her condition, the doctors could do little to help her and she died.

The idea of anyone in the United States starving to death is appalling, but this woman's story is all the more shocking because of an ironic discovery the authorities made. Routinely investigating her life, they learned this "poor" woman had eight hundred thousand dollars in local savings accounts in addition to enough IT&T stock to give her a total financial worth of more than one million dollars! Yet in spite of the enormous resources available to her, she lived in poverty and died of malnutrition.

Why would anyone do such a thing? Was she stupid? Was she sick? Was she insane? Probably not. I think she was *afraid* — afraid to touch her resources, afraid to use them, afraid to let them go. Fear controlled her, and her vast wealth was useless.

As tragic as this woman's story may seem, I don't think it differs much from the lives of millions of people today. We all have enormous potential and resources that we will never use. If we could measure what is available to us on a scale of one to a hundred, few of us would tap into as much as 5 percent. Rarely would anyone hit 20 percent. Why?

It's because fear restrains most of us. It suppresses us and keeps us from reaching the fullest possible life. Fear holds us captive, victimizes us, causes us to hide. It immobilizes, paralyzes, and withers the human spirit. We become overly cautious and careful, avoiding risky situations and refusing to take chances. According to a recent news report, fear is the greatest single emotion influencing our lives.

What Are We Afraid Of?

What are we afraid of? For many of us, our fears fall into three categories: fear of rejection, loss, or pain. The first is *fear of rejection.* To love, we must open up. We must admit that we need others. But we're afraid of being needy. We want to be independent and self-sufficient—even if it means being lonely—because we interpret dependence as weakness. Admitting we're needy is risky because it makes us vulnerable. If we allow ourselves to be vulnerable, we turn over some of the control of our lives to someone else—someone who may abandon us or hurt us, and we don't want to risk that.

So we become self-protective. We hide ourselves by the way we behave. Sometimes we hide behind shyness, or belligerence, or manipulation. Or we try to intimidate others. By being so protective, we set ourselves up for the very thing we fear: rejection. So we allow fear to cripple our relationships.

The second category is *fear of loss.* Our most painful emotions seem to be related to our fear of losing something—or someone—special to us. To protect ourselves from loss, we become possessive, clinging anxiously to whatever item or person is important to us. Our possessiveness can apply to people, to things, even to ideas.

For some of us the possession we clutch the most is our money. Thinking it will keep us secure or solve our problems, we cannot part with it unless it is to control others or buy us more security.

Others of us can't seem to release our children. We disapprove of the mates they select. We continually bail them out of problems so they cannot mature and develop a sense of responsible independence. We insist they select careers that match our desires for them—even if those careers don't match our children's skills or interests.

Some of us embrace traditions that offer a sense of security in a time of rapid change, or else we adopt farfetched philosophies in hopes of escaping the realities that confront us daily. Some invest in great works of art to give them a feeling of importance, while many cling to material possessions to prove to themselves that they are successful.

Tied into this possessiveness is the fear of whatever emotion or experience will follow the loss. For example, if I fear losing my job, I may also fear the experience of poverty as well as the emotions of embarrassment and disgrace.

Consider the two following lists, which reveal some of the aspects of life that we most commonly try to possess:

POSSESSION	*If lost*	FEAR
Reputation		Humiliation
Position		Disgrace
Power or Control		Being Used or Manipulated
Job or Ability		Poverty
Health		Illness, Weakness
Independence		Dependence
Life		Death/the Ultimate Loss

There are, of course, many other fears. And it seems obvious that we cannot live without fear and be possessive. If we possess nothing, we can lose nothing; if we can lose nothing, we cannot be afraid.

When the Falkland Islands were invaded by Argentines, I noticed this paragraph in one of the first news reports in the *Los Angeles Times:*

Marine Maj. Michael Norman, one of two officers who took part in the battle said: "It was a very frightening experience—10 yards away from them for about 10 minutes. We all very quickly came to terms with the fact that we would probably die within the next half hour. I certainly did. *Once you came to terms with that, the feeling of fear disappeared and you got on with the job."* [Italics mine.]

Fear Possesses, Love Releases

The substance that holds things together in our lives is either fear or love. If you want to know what really ties you to another person, there is a simple way to find out. Just release the other person and let them go. If your emotions choke you at the thought, and inside you're saying, *But I can't! I love you . . . you're mine . . . you belong to me . . . after all I did for you,* then fear is what holds the relationship together.

But if your response allows the other person freedom, your relationship is cohesive because of love. Fear possesses, love releases. When we seek to possess someone, we smother them, crush them, take away their life. Any relationship or system (political or religious) that depends on fear for survival is a failure. There is probably nothing more sinister and dangerous than a fearful, possessive system operating under the guise of love and freedom.

IF YOU LOVE SOMETHING

SET IT FREE.

IF IT COMES BACK TO YOU, IT'S YOURS,

IF IT DOESN'T, IT NEVER WAS.

When we see something or someone we like, our natural impulse is to want it, to want to possess it. The need to possess comes from the idea that we can guarantee that what we like will be around tomorrow for us to enjoy. But the possessiveness (fear) of today negates any possible enjoyment—and tomorrow never comes. We cannot enjoy what we possess, because of the overriding fear of losing it.

Love Is a Nonpossessive Delight

I can remember occasions when my wife would admire a beautiful dress in a window, and, noticing this, I would suggest that she buy it. The idea was that if you see something you like, you should have it. But she was content just to admire it.

We must love things enough to enrich our lives while we have them—not enough to impoverish our lives when they are gone. The things of creation are intended to arouse delight without fully satisfying desire. We should offer neither contempt nor worship to things.

A great lover is one who releases. He is able to release because he has been released. He realizes that he doesn't even own his own life. He has nothing to lose. He is able to freely give himself away. Otherwise, he will be possessive and defensive of his ego, his reputation, his position, and so on.

The third fear that haunts us is our *fear of pain.* When we can't avoid it, we try to eliminate it—to get relief. The United States pharmaceutical industry produces nearly eleven thousand metric tons of aspirin every year for domestic use, and there are more than a thousand aspirin-based pain relievers on the market.

For relief of emotional pain, many turn to tranquilizers, for which physicians write more than sixty million prescriptions yearly. Often these drugs are used by people who need help to cope with the everyday stresses of life. Add to that the millions of Americans who are afflicted with alcoholism, and our frantic attempts to escape pain become shockingly clear.

Nonetheless, we seem unable to resolve the problem of pain. Whether we live or whether we die, pain is an inevitable part of the human condition. We cannot choose whether or not we will experience pain, but we can choose our attitude toward it.

We can choose to allow pain to alert us to the needy areas of our lives, to warn us of danger, to sensitize us to the pain of others, to help us grow. When we allow fear of pain to keep us from growing, we deteriorate.

Whether I deteriorate or whether I grow, *something* must hold my life together, must motivate me, must stimulate me. That cohesive substance will be one of two things: either fear or love.

I WILL EITHER LOVE OR PERISH— I CHOOSE TO LOVE

To better understand the relationship between fear and love, let's draw a parallel between darkness and light. Let's assume that most of my life I have been living and working in the dark. Not only has it been difficult to be productive, it has also been painful and destructive because I continually bump into and fall over things.

I keep thinking, *There must be a better way.* Then somebody tells me there *is* a better way, and that "way" is to get rid of the darkness. But how do I do that? Well, I can get angry at the darkness, swear at the darkness, spit on the darkness, and punch the dark air with my fists, but it will not go away; none of these will effect any change. To my knowledge, there is only one way to banish darkness, and that is to turn on the light.

The Secret Is to Get the Light On

Curiously, we define darkness as the absence of light. We don't say light is the absence of dark. No one enters a room and says, "There's not much dark in here." We talk, rather, in terms of how much light there is. Why? Because darkness cannot be measured. Yet we know that if we turn on a little bit of light, we'll get rid of a little bit of darkness. The more light we turn on, the less darkness there will be. It's cause and effect.

You probably hadn't thought about it, but you don't have to work at keeping the darkness on. Darkness is the natural state. Darkness is relentless. To overcome the darkness we must keep lighting candles. We can never take the light for granted. Getting rid of the darkness is not the secret. If I will turn on the light, the light by its very nature will eliminate the darkness. To paraphrase a famous quote: The penalty that we pay for indifference to the light is to be enveloped by the darkness. Light candles!

Similarly, the way to a better life is not to eliminate fear, but to replace it with something better. Imagine, for example, that the leaders of your community decided to lift every law and restraint for twenty-four hours. No traffic laws. No police patrols. No law enforcement. No rules or regulations on the job or on the campus. All persons could do *what* they pleased, *how* they pleased, *where* they pleased, and *to whom* they pleased.

What would the results be? Probably all hell would break loose. We seem to need laws—and the fear of getting caught—to keep us from destroying ourselves and to protect us from each other . . . *until we learn to love.*

There is a commercial for the TV program "People's Court," which says, "The only thing that stands between man and the jungle is the law." I would like to add, "or love." Until there is love, there must be fear. We do have a choice of fear or love. Civilization may be nothing more than a thin veneer of restraint.

One example of how fear of the law motivates us occurred to me a few years ago when we decided to add some rooms to our house. Our dreams became a plan, and our plans became a blueprint. The blueprint was there to tell the builders how to put everything together properly. Finally, there was a building code with certain requirements spelled out to make sure everything was structurally sound.

We hired a contractor, who hired framers, plumbers, roofers, electricians. After every phase was completed, we had to call out the city building inspector. Why did we need an inspector? Didn't the builders understand how to read blueprints and follow the building code? Why couldn't they just come in, do their jobs, and let us know when they were finished? It wasn't long before I knew the answer.

As in the majority of building projects, there were several

delays. In most cases, what do you think caused the delay? People usually want to blame the inspector. But that was not the case with us.

One man left out a bar of steel to cut costs, hoping that no one would notice. But the inspector noticed and instructed him to go back and do it right. Delay. A plumber bent one of the pipes and figured he could get by if no one noticed. The inspector noticed. Another delay.

Those who were responsible for the delays were hoping to beat the code. Expediency overshadowed the possible consequences of ignoring what they knew was right. I think there is a lesson in this story to help us to discover whether we are motivated by fear or love. Consider this:

WOULD YOU DO IT RIGHT THE FIRST TIME . . .
EVEN IF THERE WERE NO INSPECTOR?

If you would, you're motivated by love. If not, you are motivated by fear. Similar to the builders, we all know what the "code" of life is; it's built into our conscience. We all know how to be fair to one another. Whether or not we can quote it accurately, we all understand the essence of the Golden Rule: treat others as you want to be treated. But all human failure is the result of lack of love. Until we choose love, we have no option but to live with fear.

THERE IS NO FEAR IN LOVE

This puts us in a dilemma. We understand that the way to eliminate fear is with love, but the irony is, love scares us! It's risky. It hurts. It makes us vulnerable. It demands that we release what we're afraid of losing. It confronts us with reality, just as light forces us to see what is in the dark.

Choosing love can be a painful experience, because it makes us face ourselves. Personal exposure is usually uncomfortable. Why? Because we're afraid that if people *really* knew us, they would reject us; they wouldn't love us—and that is frightening.

What is our choice, then? We can try to get the light off again. Pretend we didn't see anything. Deny. Distort. Rationalize. Stay in the dark. Choose not to know. It often is easier to stay in the darkness. Many people would rather live with the problem than accept the responsibility of the solution.

Recently I was sitting in the lobby of a hotel. Someone was explaining to the woman behind the desk about a new machine that had been installed. I heard her say, "Don't tell me about the machine. If I know about it, you will hold me responsible to run it."

She was afraid to make mistakes, afraid to assume responsibility, afraid to step out of the familiar. She chose the darkness. There really is a degree of bliss in ignorance, but it's debilitating. You can be like the woman in the hotel and choose to remain in the dark. If you do, however, you will probably continue to buy into the system based on fear, and you'll miss the adventure of being a great lover.

But, if you decide to act upon the principles presented throughout this book, you will begin to see yourself differently. You will affirm your strengths and become aware of new areas for growth as the candles are lit. It will not be easy, and it will make you uncomfortable, but the tension will cause new growth.

No Pain, No Gain

Growing takes effort. I was reminded of that truth recently at the health club where I am a member. Three times a week I head over to the gleaming chrome body-building machines for a workout. An instructor is there to observe me and to help me do the correct number of knee bends, arm curls, and sit-ups.

One day I struggled through my quota of thirty knee bends and prepared to step down when the instructor said, "Do one more." "I don't think I can." "Try it," he urged. I struggled and strained and did one more. "That's the only one that did you any good," the instructor chuckled. "No pain, no gain."

The subtle danger of such an operation is that I can fool myself into believing I am making progress just by going through the motions. I could take pride in the idea that I attend an exercise club three times a week, but without struggle, the workouts have very little or no value. The value, the growth, the improvement, comes from stretching the muscle.

Similarly, spiritual and emotional growth comes the same way. The emotional tension and challenge of a problem will make us stronger if we hang in there and learn from what we experience. In a sense, you are faced with that choice as you read these pages.

In the following chapters, you will see how to turn on the light of love. How to be responsible for your own feelings. How to motivate people to be all they were intended to be. How to be a great lover. Which way will you choose to live? Will you be motivated by law and fear, or will you live from a foundation of love? The only thing you have to lose is fear.

Step Two to Becoming a Great Lover: Make a conscious decision to release everything and everybody you perceive you possess; experience a *nonpossessive delight!*

Workshop:

1. Go back to the Values Inventory and check on how you answered question 5, "What is the finest compliment someone can give you?" and question 10, "What do you think motivates you?" Since we are motivated by our values, see if you have been aware of how much your answer to 5 is a motivating fac-

tor in your life. And on 10, see if you can reduce your answer to the common denominator of love or fear.

2. List the things and people that you are aware of trying to possess and see if you are willing to release them.
3. What are some advantages of staying in the dark?
4. What is the best way to discover if we are motivated by fear or love?
5. How can we discover whether love or fear holds our relationships together?

3

How to Really *Be Somebody*

One symbol of how the system perpetuates its propensity for creating failures can be found in most school annuals. I recently looked through the pages of a high school yearbook to see if they were still making dedications to the "most likely." Sure enough, I found several full-page, full-color dedications to the "somebodies" on campus. This is a partial list. Pay close attention to the superlatives:

> Most Likely to Succeed
> Most Athletic
> Best Dancer
> Smartest
> Most Liked
> Best Body
> Most Romantic
> Best Looking

In comparing ourselves to a list like that, most of us are likely to have a feeling of inferiority—of being a nobody. After dealing with thousands of people in seminars across the country, I've come to the conclusion that most of us do not feel esteemed, worthy, or loved. Various studies in self-esteem seem to support my observation, because they indicate that by the time most children reach adolescence, they feel inferior.

In his book *Preparing for Adolescence,* Dr. James Dobson, Associate Clinical Professor of Pediatrics at the University of Southern California School of Medicine, says that *most* teenagers decide they lack the necessary ingredients for dignity and worth, and they make this decision between the ages of thirteen and fifteen. They conclude they are truly inferior!

Is there a difference between *being* inferior and *feeling* inferior? In one sense, there is a very real difference. If I were truly inferior, nothing could be done about it. If I only *feel* inferior, I can do a lot to *change* my feelings.

But in another sense, there is little difference between being and feeling inferior. Because my feelings of inferiority are very real to me, I am going to *act as if* I were truly inferior.

Opening a seminar one day, I asked, "What kind of personality do you think you have?" A woman in the front row replied, "Lousy!"

I am sure she made a correct assessment about her *feelings.* I am just as sure she was incorrect about the *facts.* She was not a lousy person. Because she saw herself as having a lousy personality, she behaved in a "lousy" manner. And, of course, the lousy behavior proved what she believed about herself. Our behavior does not prove what kind of person we are; it affirms the way we see ourselves. And the cycle continues.

There is only one way to initiate inferiority feelings, and that is to make a comparison. When we make comparisons, we will always find someone who looks better, or knows more, or does better than we do. By comparison, we feel inferior.

To handle these negative feelings, we try to compensate by becoming critical, judgmental, and proud, which is supposed to make us feel superior. Either way—whether with inferior attitudes or superior attitudes—we lose because of the damage these attitudes foster in our relationships with others.

Low self-esteem will express itself as either false humility or false pride. Healthy self-esteem accepts its equal value with others.

Superior to Others=False Pride
Equal to Others=Healthy Self-Esteem
Inferior to Others=False Humility

I am not better than you. I am not less than you. I am me—
and that's good enough! Egotism, vanity, and conceit which
we are constantly suspecting in one another are really the very
opposite of true self-love, self-acceptance, self-esteem, and self-
celebration.

HUMILITY IS TO CHOOSE
TO BE KNOWN FOR WHO I REALLY AM—
NO MORE AND NO LESS

We are all equal, speaking of the inherent value in every person. All are equal and whether or not you believe this will be a
test of your humility. To negate or deny our inherent value as
human beings is not an act of humility.

But the system doesn't want us to be satisfied with who we are.
Instead, they urge us to continue making comparisons with others
in an effort to find out who we are. Let's look at three standards of
comparisons that have been set up: how we *look;* what we *know;*
and what we *achieve.*

False Standard #1—How We Look

From the moment we are born, the system teaches us that how
we look is important. One of the first things a new mother wants
to know is "How does the baby look?" She carefully unwraps the
blankets and counts the fingers and toes and tries to decide who
the baby resembles. But what do you say to a mother whose baby
isn't really all that pretty? You might try, "He looks just like his
father."

Even our earliest childhood literature complies with the system, teaching us that beauty is an important condition to being accepted and making it in life. Perhaps you know the story of the Ugly Duckling. Of course, being ugly was only part of his rejection experience.

Early in his journey, he ran into some birds that could fly, and because he could not perform as they, he was rejected. Then the farmer's wife brought him inside hoping he could lay some eggs. But naturally, *he* could not lay eggs, and again because he did not perform as expected, he was cast aside.

The story has a happy ending, though. The duckling finally made a delightful discovery: He had become a beautiful swan, winning the unfailing admiration of all those who had once ridiculed and rejected him. How many young people share a similar fantasy, waiting painfully for their beautiful swan-self to emerge? But it never does—even though they try to help it along with cosmetics, hair spray, and the latest fad.

More recently, a fourth-grade reader was adopted as a California textbook. The book carried a fairy story about three little girls. Two of the girls were attractive, having beautiful hair and facial features. Because of their beauty, they were loved by the people and were given their own kingdoms to rule.

The third little girl was ugly. No one liked her because she was unpleasant to look at, and no one wanted her to have her own kingdom. She was miserable and lonely until one day she was given a kingdom with the animals. This gave the story a happy ending, but the tragedy remained. As it often does, "ugliness" banished a human being from the world of "normal" people. The message is clear: To be esteemed and worthy, one must be beautiful.

Recently I attended a dinner party where the guests were discussing the tragic death of a young preschooler. During the conversation, one woman kept saying, "But she was such a beautiful baby!" I found myself wondering, *Would that child's parents have experienced a lesser grief or a milder pain had their little girl not been so pretty?*

From all directions, the absurdity of the standard bombards us: the twenty-billion-dollar cosmetic industry; ultrathin fashion models; grammar school children dressed in designer clothing; the rise of health spas and the emphasis on body building. The system screams the message: "To be loved, valued, successful, and worthy, you've got to be one of the beautiful people!"

Yet most of us are flawed. We're not ugly, not grotesque, not homely. We're just average, ordinary people with average, ordinary bumps and scars. How can our looks ever define who we are?

The standard of how we look fails because it is based on something temporary. There is no universal, timeless aspect to human fashion and beauty. If we build our lives on the platform of our looks, we will inevitably discover the platform is really a scaffold, and time is the hangman.

False Standard #2—What We Know

The second standard the system sets for being somebody is what we know. The more we know, the more we are. If we really want to be somebody, we've got to be smart.

I have discovered that if you tell people they are bad, they really don't care. If you tell them they are immoral, it doesn't bother them. But if you tell them they are dumb—they care! The number one put-down in our society is to call somebody a dummy or an idiot.

In one of my seminars I asked students to respond to the statement, "I feel intelligent." Before I could explain how I wanted them to answer, one woman blurted, "That depends upon who I'm with!" I'm sure we've all had the experience of being around somebody really "smart" and feeling "dumb" by comparison. Then, of course, we have to look around for someone who doesn't know as much as we do, so we can feel smart again.

If my IQ is 100 and yours is 130, you're obviously 30 points "better" than I am. If that threatens my self-image, I will do everything in my power to raise my IQ to 130 in order to be just as "good" as you are. (Chances are, I would probably try for 131 because I am not satisfied to be your equal. What I really want is to be better!)

Because intelligence is so relative, it's really impossible to make comparisons—but how we try! We seem to bow at the shrine of intellect. We are awed by Ph.D.'s. We give so much credence to what people are supposed to know, that we find it difficult to understand when educated people do "dumb" things and get into trouble. On the other hand, a person can be a moral reprobate, but if he has a string of degrees behind his name, somebody will stand in awe and think his education or his IQ make up for his behavior.

I wonder if there is a child in your city who hasn't been told, "If you really want to be somebody, you've got to get an education; you've got to go to school." Teachers often give the unspoken message, "I'm not going to care about you unless you are a good student in my class." Educators perpetuate the problem by maintaining an outdated, comparative grading system. Does the earning of A's or D's really determine who a child is?

How many thousands have worked hard to get that education and discovered that they still don't feel good about themselves? Our streets are full of educated derelicts. I'm not knocking education—we need all the truth we can get. But the danger lies in believing we must get an education in order to be somebody.

The standard of what we know fails because it is founded on the misconception that our worth is based on our capacity to be omniscient. Will Rogers said, "Everybody is ignorant; just on different subjects." John Kennedy added, "The greater our knowledge increases, the greater our ignorance unfolds."

It's okay to want to know all we can, and it's also okay not to know everything. Most important is not to allow our self-worth to be determined by what we know in comparison to the knowledge of others.

False Standard #3—What We Do

The most deadly of society's standards is the one that says we are somebody because of what we *do*. It's almost an equation: WHAT YOU DO=WHAT YOU ARE. It means our *right to be* is determined by our *ability to do,* and our worth is measured in terms of performance.

Imagine thinking about Thomas Edison without considering the light bulb. Or Thomas Jefferson without the Declaration of Independence. Or Madame Curie without the discovery of X rays. Our identities are so interwoven with what we do that we think of ourselves in terms of our jobs or our roles.

What is the single most-asked question at parties? "What do you do?" We type people automatically by their responses. Our system of comparisons instantly pigeonholes people, often before we've learned their names.

Recently a junior high school sponsored a Parent–Kid Social. Those who attended were divided into small groups, where the teenagers were asked to identify some quality about their parents. Without exception, the students described their parents in terms of performance: She takes me shopping. He drives me to school. He's an engineer. She's a seamstress.

If all we are is what we do, what is to become of us when we are no longer able to perform? What happens to the woman who builds her role identity on being mother to her children? When those children mature and move out on their own, she no longer knows who she is.

Consider the university professor who takes a sabbatical leave—but panics when he can no longer rely on his position for his sense of worth. Or the athlete whose performance level drops. He finds himself wondering who he is when the reporters begin to clamor after the new rookie.

The standard that says our self-worth is determined by what we do is the most deadly because efficiency becomes society's number one value. And unless society is knit together with love there is only efficient organization; and when efficiency is the highest value, persons are transformed into things whose value is their contribution to making things run. Without love, efficiency can excuse everything; the weak, the voiceless, the unborn may all be sacrificed at the altar of efficiency.

The standard of what we do will always fail us because none of us can perform perfectly all the time. We are *more* than what we do. We are *more* than what we know. We are *more* than what we look like, and we are *more* than what we have.

The system will always fail us because it is false. It holds out false gods to us and suggests that we can become gods ourselves. We worship those gods daily, but they cannot meet our needs. They cannot give us fulfillment. They cannot tell us who we are. They cannot answer the question, "Can an average, ordinary-looking person with no college degree ever amount to anything—ever really *be* somebody?"

I think there is an answer. I think the answer is a resounding YES! The system has people in a stranglehold, but they can break away. They can stop buying into the system's game. A major step may be to simply: **STOP COMPARING**. We can really learn to be somebody—we can become great lovers—offering others love and affirmation so they can break free, too.

I WAS BORN AN ORIGINAL
I WON'T DIE A COPY

A great lover has a good self-concept and can accept his body without feeling uneasy about its distinctive features. He can enjoy his accomplishments without being conceited. He can view his shortcomings as problems to be overcome, rather than judge himself as a bad person or as less than someone else when he is unable to meet a standard. He can optimistically view his own mistakes by saying, "I can do better next time."

A great lover functions because he knows he *is*. He is not always trying to *become*. In the next chapter we will discuss the difference between these two functions.

Step Three to Becoming a Great Lover: Stop comparing and accept the fact that I am an original.

Workshop:

1. Check back to the Values Inventory and compare how you answered questions 4, 5, 8, 11, and 16. The key is to find out how often you referred to "doing" or "achieving." This will indicate how much you have bought into the performance syndrome of the system.
2. Who have you most often compared yourself to, in each of the three categories? Try to get in touch with whether it has made you feel inferior or superior.
3. How do you feel about the educational grading system?
4. Try to describe yourself or your children without mentioning looks, brains, or achievements.

4

The Things We Do for Love

Early in life we begin to learn the relationship between love and performing up to standards. I recently heard a university professor (who identified himself as having been "achievement obsessed") tell the following story. On several occasions, his little daughter has come bounding down the stairs in the morning, cheerily greeting him with, "Good morning, Daddy!" Absorbed in his newspaper, he mumbles a response without even looking up. On another morning, we have the same scene with the little girl's greeting virtually ignored as the father mumbles in his oatmeal. Then one morning she comes bounding down the stairs with a slightly different theme, "Morning, Daddy! Guess what? I can tie my shoes!" Immediately he sets down his paper, exclaiming, "That's great; that's Daddy's little girl," praising her with hugs and kisses. And the lesson begins to register: *Being is not enough;* it's *performance* that gets attention.

Then, in school the message continues. Billy comes home with a "bad" grade card. His father expresses his disappointment with, "Look at this grade card; you've disgraced your father." Again, the message registers: To be accepted, I've got to meet the standard. To be loved, I've got to perform up to somebody's expectations. So, fairly early in life, most of us put together what relationships are all about: "The *better* I perform, the *more* I am loved; and the *worse* I perform, the *less* I am loved. My relationships are determined by and dependent upon my ability to perform up to somebody's standard." It might be helpful to understand that this is where most of our insecurities come from: being loved when we're "good" and not being loved when we're "bad."

So, *does* the earning of A's or D's determine the kind of person we are? Not really. But which is easier to brag about? I don't imagine you've ever heard a parent say, "I've got the neatest kid in the world, she just flunked nearly everything! I'm so proud of her. She's a chip off the old block!"

Here is the problem in trying to build relationships based on performance. It is very difficult for us to *feel good* about somebody who doesn't *do good*—at least in our judgment. It looks like this:

> I do good—you feel good about me=acceptance
> I do bad—you feel bad about me=rejection

It is very difficult to build a lasting relationship that is based on how we feel about somebody's behavior.

How often do we fail to measure up to somebody's standard—even our own? And how do we feel when we fail to measure up? Unloved. And what do we do when we feel unloved? We criticize, complain, and do stupid things that "prove" that we don't deserve to be loved in the first place. And the cycle continues. When we do not feel loved, we put ourselves down and do hateful destructive things to ourselves.

Self-hate is the strongest human antihealing agent in existence. Its potential for destruction is almost limitless. Self-hate is when we hate any aspect of ourselves and whenever we have feelings of self-contempt. Any distortion of ourselves, either degrading or idealizing, must be viewed as rejection. Exaggerated opinions as to our abilities or achievements is therefore self-hate. Just as minimizing and ignoring our abilities, rather than being acts of humility, are really just other forms of self-hate.

Dr. Theodore Rubin, in his book *Compassion and Self-Hate,* says,

> I believe that so-called accidental deaths due to drug overdoses or auto mishaps of alcoholic origin or heart attacks and cerebro-

vascular accidents (strokes) associated with overeating are not accidents at all. These represent acute attacks on oneself due to feelings of unbearable self-loathing, precipitating the desire for vengeful punishment of self and permanent escape from the pain incurred. Though the immediate satisfactions derived from food and smoking are apparent and the destructive effects are not, the individual, nevertheless, does know of these latter effects. Unconscious self-hate sustains these habits.

Be Compassionate With Yourself

When we fail to meet the standard and feel the self-hate coming on, we must learn to be compassionate with ourselves.

Learning to be compassionate with ourselves does not mean that we overlook and ignore errors, mistakes, and unacceptable behavior. For instance, I trust that my children know that I cannot and will not ever love them any more or less than I do right now. My love does not come and go with their behavior. The key is being committed to the relationship. The child is going to do things that I approve of, and we will discuss it—but not in the context of love or relationship. There will be times when the child does things that I disapprove of, that are socially unacceptable, or that are not in his best interests and, again, the particular behavior is discussed and corrected or disciplined if need be, but not in the context of love or relationship.

Several years ago we lived in a house with a profusion of flowers in the backyard. Because there were so many, the children were told they could do anything with them, and so they did. They would pick them to decorate doll houses and palm trees and would even try to sell them to our neighbors. All of which was okay. But we had some very special, prize roses in the front yard and the children were instructed to leave them alone. These flowers were strictly "hands off," unless someone was there to help clip them properly. (Conditions of behavior had been established.)

So what do you do when your four-year-old comes in the house with her hands behind her back, singing "Happy Birthday, Dear Daddy"? She says, "Close your eyes. I've got a surprise." So I closed my eyes and did she have a surprise! She produced a handful of rosebuds, all broken off at the base. She placed them in my hands with the words "I love you, Daddy!" Now that's what you might call a problem. How do you handle it? The chances are if you get sentimental you will not handle it properly. Understanding the difference between being and doing will help.

My response sounded something like this: "Celeste, I love you, too. You are a very special girl. You are thoughtful, considerate, and loving." (What I have done up to now is talk about *who she is,* affirming the relationship.) Then I proceeded to discuss what she had *done.*

"However, you did something I told you not to do, didn't you?"

"Yes," she replied.

"What did I say I would do if you did that?"

She told me.

I asked her, "What do you think I ought to do?"

She wasn't sure!

I paddled her (just a little) as I had promised. I had to, for her sake, so she would know she could trust me to keep my word. I did my best to affirm our relationship and who she was before I disciplined what she did. She knew the difference. Love for the *person* is *unconditional.* Discipline of *behavior* must always be *conditional.*

So, in business, people must often be disciplined or let go. There are certain rules that are necessary to get the job done, for example, being on time. If a person deliberately and continually fails to keep the rules, discipline may be necessary, and ultimately you may have to let him go. It's not necessary to call him names, such as incompetent, lazy, incorrigible. Just deal with the conditions he has chosen not to meet and leave intact what esteem he has.

Notice these differences in referring to personage or behavior.

"You're a liar."	Personage
"You didn't tell the truth, did you?"	Behavior

"You are really stupid."	Personage
"That wasn't the smart thing for you to do, was it?"	Behavior
-------------------	
"You are so clumsy."	Personage
"I see the milk got spilled. Here's a cloth you can use to wipe it up."	Behavior

Living Up to Our Images

We have a way of living up to our images. We perform according to how we see ourselves and how others see us. I remember a woman who kept calling her son Dennis the Menace. I asked her why she called him that and she replied, "Because that's the way he behaves." I suggested, "Maybe he behaves that way because of what you call him."

At the conclusion of a recent seminar, a man asked for permission to drive me to the airport. He informed me he had a personal problem that he wished to discuss with me and thought this would give us a few minutes alone. I agreed to the arrangement, and we left for the airport. I had hardly settled in the seat when he said, "I have this twenty-three-year-old son who is a born loser and I'd like to find a way to help him." Perhaps you reacted to that statement the same way I did. How do you treat a person you perceive to be a born loser?

After a little discussion, I said to the man, "I'd like to ask you a question. How do you think your son sees himself in your eyes?" After a pause, he thoughtfully replied, "That's it, isn't it?" And I said, "Yes, I think that's it. If you would see him differently, you would treat him differently."

In the words of Goethe, "If I treat you as you are, you will remain as you are. If I treat you as if you were what you could be, that is what you will become." That is an act of faith—to see people's potential.

About twenty-five years ago, Dr. Henrietta Mears said to me, "David, you will not be influenced by people you believe in nearly as much as you will be influenced by people who believe in you." Do you have anyone who believes in you? Anyone who is really pulling for you, who really wants you to make it? That's a powerful force in our lives.

You Are Not What You Do

When we learn to separate who people are from what they do, we can stop one of the biggest hindrances to love: judging people by what they do. When we are disappointed with the performance of another individual, we are faced with a decision—to accept them, in spite of what they do, or evaluate them because of what they do.

For example, last year I did a staff development seminar for a high school. The seminar was scheduled to end at 4:30 in the afternoon.

When I arrived at the school, the principal informed me that some of the teachers might leave at 4:00 because union rules say they are not required to stay any longer. They could stay if they wanted to, but the principal could not require it.

At about 3:55, I noticed some of the teachers begin to shuffle their papers. At 3:57 they closed their notebooks. At 3:59 they put on their coats. The clock in the room was one of those that jumps the minutes, and when that hand went straight up to 4:00, ten teachers left the room. Now tell me, what kind of teacher would leave the room at straight up 4:00 when the seminar wasn't scheduled to end until 4:30?

Notice what I have done. I've set you up to make a judgment.

Did you? A judgment says, because of what they *did*—they left before the seminar was over—they must *be* rude, or discourteous, or bored, or whatever. However, we can't be sure of any of those motives. The only thing we know for sure is that at 4:00 ten teachers left the room. Period.

I ACKNOWLEDGE WHAT IS WITHOUT
MAKING VALUE JUDGMENTS

I was recently standing in line in a supermarket with about a dozen items in my basket. Being next to check out, I moved toward the register. As I did, a woman came running up behind me and said, "I have only one item and I'm kind of in a hurry. Would you mind if I go ahead of you?" I replied, "Yes, I would mind. I'm next and I think it will be all right for you to wait your turn."

Now, what kind of a person would do something like that? If you think that what I did was assertive, courageous, and strong, you would probably judge me to be a great person.

If, on the other hand, you think what I did was discourteous, selfish, and inconsiderate, you would probably judge me to be a terrible person.

Using your standard of "good" and "bad," you would take about thirty seconds of my life to decide what kind of person you think I am. Either way, you do not really know. All you know for sure is that I didn't allow someone to go in front of me.

I remember hearing Zig Ziglar tell a story about a father who was traveling at night on a train. In one of the coaches the father was pacing, carrying a small, crying baby who was obviously disturbing several passengers.

One irritated man finally blurted, "Why don't you shut that baby up, or give it to its mother so we can get some sleep!"

With a break in his voice, the father replied, "I'd love to give him to his mother, but she's in a coffin in the car behind this one. We're taking her home to bury her."

The irritated man was humbled. With tears in his eyes, he dropped to his knees asking the father to forgive him. He said, "I'm sorry. *I didn't know.* Why don't you let me carry the child for a while, so you can get some rest."

You Never Have Enough Information to Make a Judgment

If, as a salesperson, you are making judgments, you will narrow your clientele to the kind of people you like, and that will hardly be enough for you to survive, either personally or professionally. If you're not judging and are committed to meeting your clients' needs, regardless of how you feel about things they do that you don't like, the whole world is your clientele!

One of the main reasons that making judgments is such a hindrance to relationships is because it leads to resentment and an unforgiving spirit. Resentment is wanting the other person to feel guilty or bad. It is suppressed anger and hostility. It's an unwillingness to let the other person change. This leads to an unwillingness to forgive, which is a form of vengeance, where we end up being like what we hate, as we seek to hurt for the same reason we were hurt. It's an unwillingness to let go, to give up control.

If the love seems shut off in your life, it may be because you have decided not to love in one of these ways. You have the power to start the love flowing in your life again. Forgiveness keeps love flowing. When we truly love people, we do not require them to make up for their every mistake. The higher our standards are the higher our forgiveness must be.

Don't Look for Justice—Give It!

We probably live in the most litigious society in history. A litigious society is an unforgiving society. We won't allow people to make mistakes. We will not give a second chance. When we are not allowed mistakes, we're certainly not going to take many risks because we don't dare fail. When we are afraid to take risks, most creativity and adventure come to a halt in business, education, and personal relationships.

To get things moving again we've got to have some great lovers who are willing to forgive. It doesn't matter whether people love us—*we love them.* It does not matter if people understand us—*we understand them.* And even if they do not forgive us, *we forgive them.* Do not look for justice in this world. But never fail to give it!

I think that this matter of forgiveness is so essential to loving relationships that we need to look a little closer at the process. Is it possible to forgive and not forget? Yes, but if we have truly forgiven, we will never bring it up again. The Bible tells us that God does forget when He forgives us.[1] But we are not God. We find it difficult to forget, and sometimes memories surface from our subconscious minds when we think we *have* forgotten. How, then, can we be certain that we have forgiven?

Here is a test: If I should tell you something wonderful about someone you feel wronged you, you will not feel any resentment. You have forgiven that person if you are glad and *wish him well.* The memory will be there, but the pain and anger and resentment will be gone.

Perhaps you have been struggling in one of your relationships. Your feelings of anger, pain, and resentment have shut off the flow of love. If you are serious about getting the love flowing again, here is a meditation with which you can begin:

> I fully and freely forgive (mention the name of the person). I release him/her mentally and spiritually. I completely forgive everything that was done. I am free, and he/she is free. I feel relieved. I wish for him/her health, happiness, peace, and all the blessings of life. I do this joyously and lovingly. Whenever I think of him/her I say, "I release you and all the blessings of God are yours. I forgive you as I have been forgiven. Amen.

---

1. *See* Jeremiah 31:34; Hebrews 8:12

MY LOVE IS UNCONDITIONAL
WHEN NOTHING IS UNFORGIVABLE

Most people I dialogue with speak of the desire to be loved unconditionally, but have seldom, if ever, experienced it. But as much as people talk about unconditional love, I suspect that most of us are in a double bind. There is no doubt that we desire to be loved, but we may want to be loved for the wrong reasons.

Conditions of Love

We may be familiar with the idea of love being either conditional or unconditional, and there seem to be at least three basic conditions.

The first condition is: *I love you if.* I will love you if you meet my standards. Or, I will accept you if you meet my conditions. If you will be nice to me, I will be nice to you. As long as you respect me, I will respect you. Have you ever heard anyone declare, "After what she did to me, see if I ever do anything nice for her again." My treatment of you becomes conditioned by your treatment of me.

The second condition is: *I love you **because** ...*

... you're beautiful or handsome
... you have a great mind
... you have power, or position, or status
... you have a great body
... you give me nice things.

The problem with this condition is that it is terribly insecure. It involves always making comparisons and being in competition with whoever comes along who is more beautiful, more brilliant, more popular, or a better performer, or has a better body.

Do you recall the Geritol ad that appeared on television a few seasons ago? The handsome but greying husband slips his arm around his lovely wife and says, "My wife takes good care of herself. She takes Geritol and I love her for it." Imagine the pressure that poor woman is under! She has to chugalug that stuff every day to keep the relationship going.

Because can also be a manipulative tool. Some people demand the love of others as payment for some expression of endearment. I know of a family whose maiden aunt showers the children with toys and candy and gifts, and then, citing her generosity, demands constant gratitude and attention.

"After all I've given you," she pouts, "you should be willing to meet me halfway. Give Auntie a hug—after all, I bought you that new doll."

Tragically, this woman's demands are driving her family farther and farther away because her "love" is used for barter and blackmail.

GENEROSITY IS GOOD DEEDS THAT ARE DONE QUIETLY, INCONSPICUOUSLY, AND ARE IMMEDIATELY FORGOTTEN

The third condition we place on our willingness to love is *I love you as soon as.* As soon as you do what I want and meet my needs, I will love you. As soon as you measure up to my standard, I will accept you. We use this condition a lot with children. As soon as you make the team, as soon as you get the grades, or as soon as you clean the room, I'll give you some attention.

The *as soon as* requirement places the burden of responsibility on the other person, whose performance then becomes the object of the "love."

Recently a couple came to my office for counseling. They were trying to save their marriage. While the husband struggled to explain his position, he said, "I just wish she would read all the books I've read, and listen to all the cassettes I've listened to, and go to all the seminars I've attended."

"Why are you interested in her doing all these things?" I asked. I'll never forget his answer: "Because I know what a wonderful woman she could be."

What did his wife hear? "I am not a wonderful being, but *as soon as* I *do* all the necessary things, I'll be loved." Because she wanted very much to be accepted by him, she felt tremendous pressure to measure up to his standard, to meet his conditions—and it was an impossible task.

For at least fifteen years of marriage I believed I was loved "because." What I also discovered was that for years, what I thought was love was nothing but barter. "If," "because," and "as soon as" have nothing to do with love. It's barter. It's an exchange.

True love is unconditional, and unconditional love says, "I love you *anyway.*" Or, "I love you *in spite of.*" Or,

I LOVE YOU FOR NO GOOD REASON

Now, how do you think your ego could handle that? When I came to the realization that I was loved "in spite of," I didn't like it. It was a blow to my ego, but it was a freeing experience. Do we really want to be loved unconditionally—for no good reason at all? I think that I, like so many others, really want to be loved for the wrong reasons. We really want to be loved because we're handsome, or pretty, or smart. We want to be loved and admired for our achievements. Our pride makes it difficult for us to accept unconditional love.

Don't we usually respond to the expression, "I love you," with a question, "Why?" Isn't that asking for a condition? The double bind is that we say we would like to be loved unconditionally, but our egos somehow want to earn it, or deserve it, or somehow qualify.

The wrong reasons for *not* being loved are because I think I am ugly, or dumb, or incapable, or bad. The right reason for being loved is that apart from God's unconditional love, I can never be all I was meant to be. Only when I have *received* and experienced unconditional love from outside the human experience am I able to *give* unconditional love.

Admit You Need Love

Have you ever considered how the biblical concept of unconditional love breaks the perform-to-be-loved syndrome?

God doesn't love us *if* we are good, or kind, or decent. He doesn't love us *because* we are moral, or honest, or religious, or generous to charities. He doesn't love us *as soon as* we are good enough to measure up. He simply loves us because He is love.

Even though His love is unconditional, there is a very large condition on our part: *We must let Him love us.* We must admit our need for God's love because we cannot go it alone. Admitting our neediness—our dependency—is perhaps the most difficult step of all.

The amazing thing is, once we receive and experience this love, we find we are free to love—to be great lovers. There is no need to work so hard to prove our self-worth. That need for feeling special has been met. WE HAVE BEAT THE SYSTEM! And when we believe this, we become achievers with delight, compassion, and gratitude. It is an effect, a by-product of our newly found selves.

When we accept our self-worth and adequacy as a gift, we immediately perceive a new standard of achievement. It is not performance but our measure of faithfulness to our gifts. Faithfulness is the only adequate, all-inclusive definition of success. And with it, no one has an excuse for not being successful.

To understand the heart of motivation is to understand how to break the perform-to-be-loved syndrome. Everything we do is done to *get* love or *because* we're loved. It looks like this:

Perform to *get*→ (LOVE) →Perform because you've *got* it.

A chart in chapter 9 will show that love includes attention, recognition, appreciation, and so on. The relentless drive to get these things is neurotic and unfulfilling. A great lover lives his life as an *expression of love,* not a vain effort to achieve it. It is not a hunger that needs to be filled, but a fullness that gives away.

So, it's time to answer the big question: "How do we get people from doing what they do to *get* love, to doing what they do *because* they're loved?" I believe this is the most important motivational truth I can give you: *Give people what they need unrelated to how they perform.* To create healthy, long-lasting motivation we begin giving people what they need unrelated to what they are doing. Let me suggest a way that you can start. As soon as you have the occasion, I want you to go up to someone you love and for no good reason, give him a big hug, and say, "I just want you to know how much I love you and appreciate you." Don't be surprised if you get one of these responses: What did I do? What did you do? What do you want? It is difficult for us to believe that we are loved for who we are. More often than not, "I love you" has meant, "Your behavior pleases me." We have seldom experienced being in the middle of behavior that was displeasing to someone and have them say, "I love you."

About a year ago I was doing a management seminar, and the classes were held weekly. The week we discussed giving people what they need, I gave an assignment to see whether this principle would work for them.

The instruction was that during the week the managers were to find one of their salespeople who wasn't performing too well and somehow give them what they needed apart from their performance. When the seminar resumed, one of the managers related this story.

The morning after the assignment, the manager had called one of his salesmen whose sales were down and invited him to lunch. The salesman's first response was, "What's wrong?" "Nothing's wrong," the manager assured him. "I just would like to have lunch with you."

Then the salesman thought, *If nothing's wrong, then he must want something from me.*

Very suspicious, the salesman went to lunch with his manager. Even though he kept waiting for his suspicions to be confirmed, he soon discovered that he indeed had done nothing wrong and there were no demands. The manager really just wanted to have lunch with him.

Realizing this, how do you suppose that salesman felt leaving that luncheon? He felt very special. He felt important. The manager had affirmed him just by wanting to be with him.

What if you were feeling needy, unloved, unappreciated? What would happen if I started giving you love? Approval? Appreciation? Recognition unrelated to anything you were doing? Maybe I would contact you every once in a while just to let you know I was thinking about you. What would you start believing?

I think you'd start believing that you were loved for who you are. What effect would that have on your performance? I think it would set you free to take risks. To take chances. To move out and go for it! Why? Because the relationship is not dependent on your performance. Win or lose—you'll still be loved!

FAILURE DOESN'T MEAN A THING WHEN YOUR RELATIONSHIP IS SECURE

I trust that by now you are beginning to understand the relationship between being and doing, between love and performance. Our alienation from Love and Life (our Creator) is one of fundamental relationship. It is a deliberate and emphatic decision to live independently of the Giver of Love and Life.

He does not pay any attention to the moral degradation of the one or the moral attainment of the other. He looks at something we do not see: our disposition. Is it a disposition of "self-realization" or self-sufficiency, or a disposition of "I am god"? Or is it the disposition of a loving person who is faithful with the gift of love and life that they have received.

Our disposition is determined by the decisions we make to love or not to love. The decision not to love is when I am determined to hold on to resentment, judgment, and an unforgiving attitude. This decision causes a disposition of darkness and death. The decision to love brings light and life.

Our twofold difficulty in *accepting* love as a gift and *giving* love as an act of the will was illustrated by such a national figure as Hans Selye, considered to be the world's leading authority on stress. In the September 1980 issue of *SUCCESS* magazine, Selye was quoted as saying, "Yet, another biblical rule, loving your neighbor as yourself, simply is not practical. It is great wisdom, and I don't intend to improve on the Bible, but one *cannot love on command.* [Italics mine.]

"So, I would change one word without changing its essence: *earn* [italics his] your neighbor's love. It is difficult to love everybody. Some people are just more lovable than others. But I can earn anybody's love. All of us can gain closer relationships."

Mr. Selye has fallen into the same trap as so many; that is, believing that love must be earned, that we must perform up to somebody's standard to be loved.

The passage that Hans Selye is referring to is found in Saint Matthew 22:35, 36, where Jesus answers the lawyer who had asked, "Which is the greatest commandment in the law?" The answer was to love God first, and your neighbor as yourself. Because love is a commandment, it has to be an act of the will. It is something that we decide to do or not to do. We can't command our feelings and emotions.

If I *knew* I loved my neighbor, how would I treat him? Having determined that, treat him that way, regardless of how you feel. Don't waste time wondering whether you feel good about someone; *act as if you did.* As soon as you do this, you will discover a great secret. When you are behaving as if you loved someone, you will presently come to love him or her with feelings. The most loving thing we do will probably be the hardest because it goes against our feelings.

G. K. Chesterton said: *"Loving* means to love the unlovable, or it is no virtue at all; *forgiving* means to pardon the unpardonable, or it is no virtue at all; *faith* means believing the unbelievable, or it is no virtue at all. And to *hope* means hoping when things are hopeless, or it is no virtue at all."

In the final analysis, the struggle between being and doing was perhaps best expressed by young Jim Elliot, who was killed by the Auca Indians he loved: "I analyzed afresh and repudiated my base desire to *do* something in the sight of men rather than *be* something in the sight of God, regardless of whether or not results are seen."

Step Four to Becoming a Great Lover: Give people love unrelated to their performance.

Workshop:

1. On the Values Inventory, check question 2 where you were asked to describe yourself. See how many were *being* words and how many were *doing* words.
2. On the Self-Esteem Exercise, see how you rated yourself on question 20: "I easily forgive; I don't bear grudges."
3. Why is it difficult to build lasting relationships based on what people do?
4. What three basic conditions do we place on our willingness to love?
5. As soon as possible, find an occasion to give someone love unrelated to what they are doing.
6. Do something loving for someone you consider "unlovely," for example, your boss, mother-in-law, son-in-law, neighbor—expecting nothing in return.
7. Do something loving for a family member—without him or her knowing you did it.

8. Give some of your money to a church or charitable organization—anonymously.

9. Be aware of an opportunity to get even or take advantage of someone—and don't.

10. Be aware of how your husband or wife see themselves in your eyes. How do your children or parents see themselves in your eyes? How do your clients or associates see themselves in your eyes? Are you unconsciously revealing your true feelings with the silent messages you are sending? Are you secretly disappointed because your child is "ordinary"? Do you think he is stupid? Was your child born during a difficult time, imposing financial and emotional stress on the family? Do you resent the freedom you have lost and the demands people place on your time and effort? Are you embarrassed when your spouse is either too loud and rambunctious or too inward and withdrawn? Can you teach a child to respect himself when you dislike him for reasons of your own?

Unit II

When Love Takes Charge

- Loving From the Inside Out

- You Are What You Think You Are

- Making Love a Habit

5

Loving From the Inside Out

One of the major factors affecting us today is stress. We all experience it. If we have a traffic violation, if one of our children becomes ill, if we are filling out our income tax, we can experience stress. Sometimes the stress is caused by what we would expect to be a happy experience—getting married, graduating from college, going on vacation. Other times it is provoked by grief-related situations such as being fired from a job, losing someone close because of death or divorce, or being involved in a serious argument.

Momentary stress can cause a person's energy and strength to increase temporarily. For this reason we occasionally hear of a young mother who is able to lift a car to save a child who is trapped beneath it, or of a volunteer who is able to return to a burning building again and again to rescue those inside.

Yet many physicians agree that prolonged, severe stress can promote illness. It can even lead to potentially fatal conditions such as cardiac arrest, stroke, cancer.

Although there are some who would like to suggest that all illness is psychological in origin, I believe it is unfair and dishonest to say to someone, "It's all in your head." Yet researchers suggest that 50 to 80 percent of our physical problems are emotionally induced. If that is true, we must learn to deal with our emotional reactions to stress.

The system tells us that dealing with our emotions is too difficult and that there are easier ways of handling stress. We can drink our pain away, or we can eliminate it (at least for the moment) with aspirin, antacid tablets, or tranquilizers—anything to get relief. The question is, do we merely want relief from symptoms—or do we want to be free of the causes?

I believe that if we truly want to be happy and free of dis-ease, we must face the feelings that our stress produces. We must face our anger, our resentment, our lack of forgiveness.

Inside or Outside the Circle?

To get an understanding of how we face these feelings, let's think of our lives as a circle.

Inside the circle is who you are. It is your mind, your will, and your emotions. It is your decisions, your thoughts, your hopes,

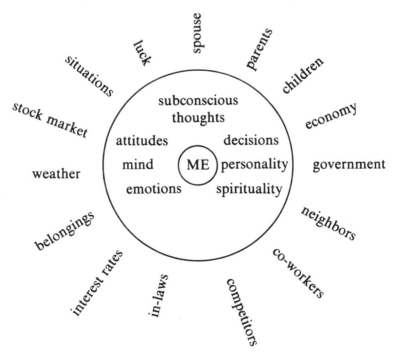

Figure 1.

and your dreams. It is your attitudes, your personality, your spirituality.

Outside the circle are all the people, places, and circumstances that can influence you, affect your life, and be a source of irritation. This could include things such as your environment, the weather, the stock market, interest rates, your mother-in-law, the government, your co-workers, and your competitors. You can probably add a few of your own.

If we truly want to be great lovers, we must ask ourselves, where is the responsibility for our attitudes, our feelings, our successes, our failures—our lives? Is it inside the circle or outside the circle? Have you, for example, ever had a crummy day? Was it really a *crummy* day? Is it possible that on that same day, another person thought it was a fantastic day? A day is a day. It's our attitude that causes us to label it as crummy or great. Rain is rain, right? If it falls on the crops . . . praises. If it falls on the picnic . . . curses. Same rain. The difference is not what it is; the difference is my attitude toward it and how I let it affect me.

But most of us spend our lives reacting to and blaming what is outside the circle. We blame everything from the weather to the economy to our parents to God. We even blame the devil himself.

Comedian Flip Wilson may have immortalized the saying, "the devil made me do it," on his television variety program, but blame has been around since fig leaves were in fashion. It began in, of all places, the perfect environment of Eden, when Adam and Eve tried to avoid the responsibility of their choices.

Sensing something was wrong, the Lord came looking for Adam, asking him what had happened to make him hide. Did Adam say, "What happened here is my fault. I take full responsibility for everything. There is no need for you to discuss this with Eve"? (And, of course, we've been following his example ever since, right?)

Most of us know the story well enough to realize that this was not Adam's response. What he really said was, "It was the *woman*, that *You* gave me. It's *Your* fault for giving her to me and it's *her* fault for giving me the stuff to eat. I am not responsible."

So, God decided to check with Eve. "What happened, Eve?" Did she accept any responsibility? No. She replied, "I was deceived. The devil made me do it. It's not my fault. I couldn't help it."

I don't know about you, but I've always had a little sympathy for Adam and Eve because they couldn't blame their environment. And they certainly couldn't blame their parents!

Since the beginning of history the problem has been the same. It has been difficult for us to face ourselves and accept responsibility for our behavior. How can we build meaningful relationships when we wear masks and put up false fronts? We want to be loved, but we're afraid that if people *really* knew us they wouldn't love us.

What's Inside Your Circle?

If you want to find out what's inside your circle, to get an insight into the kind of person you are, pay attention to the positive and negative things you either accept or reject. For now, let's call the positive things compliments and the negative things criticisms. We tend to only allow into our circles what we agree with or believe—either positively or negatively.

Let's say, for example, that you are among a group of people at a party, and someone says to you, "I've been watching you this evening. I've listened to your conversations and observed the way you relate to people. To be frank, I don't think you're being real. You seem to be acting phoney."

Try to get in touch with what you might experience at that moment. If you wanted to defend yourself in any way, if it upset you, it's because you believe it already. Therefore, you accepted it and you allowed it into your circle.

On the other hand, perhaps your response was, "No, I'm certain you made a mistake. You were probably observing someone else, because this is the way I really am. You don't know me at all." You did not entertain the idea for a moment. You dismissed it immediately because you knew it was not true of yourself, and you refused to allow it inside your circle.

The same principle works with positive input as well. Let's say that at the same party, someone approaches you and says, "I've watched you all evening, and I've listened to you. I've talked with others about you, and I think I know quite a bit about you. It seems to me that you are a warm, compassionate, loving, caring, giving individual, and I'd like to get to know you better."

How will you respond to that compliment? If you believe those things to be true, you can receive them into your circle graciously and say, "Thank you." If you react by saying, "It's getting awfully deep in here," or "Aw, you probably say that to everybody," it's because you don't believe it about yourself. You cannot allow it into your circle because it was never there in the first place. Others reflect to us what we already believe about ourselves— what is within our circles.

I ONLY LET INTO MY CIRCLE
WHAT I BELIEVE OR ACCEPT
ABOUT MYSELF

For example, if my circle is full of compassion and care and understanding and tolerance and love and consideration, and you tap into my circle, what will you get out of it? Those same positive, creative, nourishing qualities. If, on the other hand, my circle is full of anger, bitterness, greed, resentment, and jealousy, what will you receive? Anger, bitterness, jealousy—the same thing. You didn't *make* me that way; you only revealed who or what I am.

You often hear people say, "Oh, he makes me so mad!" But how about, "She makes me so kind"? Probably not! If I have any virtues, I'll accept credit for them. If I have any vices, I'd prefer to pass that responsibility on to someone else. To paraphrase Eleanor Roosevelt, No one can make you feel [*anything*] without your consent.

I AM NO BIGGER THAN WHAT IT TAKES TO UPSET ME

We're all looking for a scapegoat. We all want someone to blame. The Democrats blame the Republicans, and the conservatives blame the liberal congress. The rich blame the tax structure, and the poor blame the rich. Blacks and whites blame each other, as do husbands and wives, parents and children, brothers and sisters.

When was the last time you heard anybody say, "Hey! Guess what? I think I'm it!" One of the most important decisions we can make is to say, "I'm it. It's not somebody else that's out there; I'm it. I'm responsible for my life. It's not the weather. It's not the interest rates. It's not the government. It's me. I will no longer blame anyone or anything outside my circle. I am responsible. There is nobody to blame. From now on, I'm going to live from the inside of that circle."

I AM RESPONSIBLE FOR MY FEELINGS

I was talking to a man a few days ago who was suffering from a serious stomach disorder. That was only a symptom of his problem. His demented mother-in-law lived in his home. Don't read anything into that—she wasn't his problem either. His problem was his attitude toward her, and it was obviously eating him up. I asked him, "Would you really like to be healthy?"

"Certainly I would," he said.

"Would you really like to be happy?" I asked.

"Yes, I really would."

"Are you willing to do whatever it takes?"

"Of course!"

"All you have to do," I said, "is fall in love with your mother-in-law."

"You've got to be kidding!" he said, grasping his stomach.

Yes, I want to be happy. Yes, I want to be healthy. Yes, I want to be a success. Yes, I want to be loving. But don't ask me to be responsible for what it takes!

To my knowledge, no one ever "woke up" healthy. No one ever drifts into virtue or happiness. We are all just about as happy, healthy, virtuous, and loving as we have chosen to be. Many people would rather live with the problem than with the responsibility of the solution.

I CHOOSE MY ATTITUDE IN EVERY CIRCUMSTANCE

In the midst of the horrors of Nazi concentration camps, the famous Viennese psychiatrist Viktor Frankl observed, "Everything can be taken from man, except the last of the human freedoms, his ability to choose his own attitude in any given set of circumstances, to choose his own way."

Have you ever noticed that when you're having a full-fledged argument with your spouse or your child, the telephone invariably rings? Somebody has to answer it, so what happens? You take a 180-degree turn.

"Hi there! Oh, just fine. Never better!"

On the other end, the caller never suspects you're in the middle of a major conflict. You might even laugh, and you keep your conversation light. Then you hang up the telephone receiver. "Now! Where was I?" And the cease-fire is over.

I saw a cartoon the other day in which a little boy was saying to his mother, "Why don't you use your telephone voice with me?"

Accept What You Can't Change

In 1943, Reinhold Neibuhr wrote a little prayer that has been circulated in millions of copies. It's called the Serenity Prayer, and it really deals with living from the inside out.

> GOD, GIVE US GRACE TO ACCEPT
>   WITH SERENITY
> THE THINGS THAT CANNOT BE CHANGED,
> COURAGE TO CHANGE THE THINGS WHICH
>   SHOULD BE CHANGED,
> AND THE WISDOM TO DISTINGUISH ONE
>   FROM THE OTHER.

There are two aspects of this prayer that we can use in a very practical way. It relates to (1) things we can't change, and (2) things we can change, and, of course, the wisdom to know the difference.

Most of what we can't change is outside of the circle. We can't change the weather. We can't change certain traffic conditions. We can't change interest rates. We can't change people. What we are responsible for is our *attitude* toward these things. *That* we can change. Have you ever heard anyone come home at the end of the day with this report: "Man, am I beat. I've been fighting traffic all day."

One evening as I was traveling the freeways of Los Angeles, I had an insight: You can't fight traffic. Oh, you can get upset and fuss and yell, but it won't change anything. You won't get there any sooner. You might as well relax.

The prayer becomes even more powerful if we change just one word in the first phrase: "to accept with serenity the *people* I cannot change." Things do not bother us nearly as much as people. Most of us are guilty of trying to change others—and have probably learned that it doesn't work. What does work is to give people warmth, support, and affirmation, treating them as if they were what they could be, giving them freedom to grow and change as they choose to.

Another thing we can't change is the past. Dwelling on the hurt and guilt of the past uses up a lot of creative energy. Two words that create a lot of problems for us are *if only*. If only she hadn't done that! If only I had started sooner. If only I had followed his advice. If only I had made that investment. If only I'd never married.

Do you have any "if onlys" going? Most of us have a lot of "if onlys." There is nothing we can do about them. It's over. It's history. It's done. Close the door on it and let it go.

"But you don't know what he *did* to me," you might be saying. No, I don't know what he did to you. But I know what he's *doing* to you, and he's going to *keep* doing it to you until you let him go.

Both psychology and theology agree that there can be no healing in our life unless we are willing to release the resentments of the past, forgiving those we have been blaming—especially our parents.

Is there anything outside your circle that you have been letting bother you? Can you do anything about it? If so, bolster your courage and get to work on it. If not, **let it go.** Most of what we can change is *inside* the circle, namely ourselves, and that indeed takes a lot of courage.

You Are Responsible for Your Happiness

We don't live as isolated circles. Everyone has a circle. What happens when someone I know is living from outside his circle and blaming me for his lack of happiness? Many of us feel responsible for the happiness of other individuals. Here is good

news. *You are not responsible for anyone's happiness but your own.*
And, of course, *nobody else is responsible for your happiness.*

Does this mean that I have the right to treat somebody badly
and say, "If you're unhappy, that's your problem"? Of course not.
A great lover *cares* how other people feel, but is not responsible.
Here is where most of us are trapped. We say, "Because I care
about your happiness, I feel responsible."

I've been talking with a lot of teachers and social workers
lately, and they use a common phrase—*burn-out.* I think I know
why people burn out. It's because they have gone into the "caring
professions," and because they care, they feel the burden of responsibility. That's what burns them out. Teachers feel the responsibility for students' grades. Doctors feel the responsibility
for people's health. Clergy feel the responsibility for people's
souls. That kind of heavy responsibility burns people out. The
secret is to find the balance between caring enough to give it your
very best, but not carrying the emotional responsibility of every
person.

Now if you were to address your family today and say, "I am
no longer going to be responsible for your happiness," what
would you probably be accused of? Not caring. So don't an-
nounce it. Just don't let them hold you responsible. Anytime one
person is trying to hold another person responsible for his happiness, they are most likely in a parent–child relationship. And it
has nothing to do with age.

To help understand the balance of care and responsibility, I'll
create a hypothetical case. Let's suppose my mother were to say
to me, "Son, I cannot be happy unless you write me a letter every
week (or every month)." I'm not willing to assume a guilt trip,
so I say, "Mom, I love you, but you're going to have to learn to be
happy with or without a letter. Because I care, I'll write when I
can." Now if I really care, what will I do? I will write. But
whether I write or don't write, she is responsible for her own
happiness.

Does being responsible for my own attitudes mean that I am to
go through life rigidly, controlled, protected—not *having* feel-

ings? Of course not. We're not isolated. We all experience pain and grief and sorrow, joy and happiness. Everything outside the circle can affect us, but it's not decisive.

It's normal and appropriate and healthy to grieve, to weep, to laugh, to sing. Denying our feelings is not the same as dealing with them.

Last year, one of my children's kittens got out of the house, ran across the street, and was killed by a car. I think I would have been disappointed if she had come swinging into the house, saying, "Hey, Dad. Guess what? That dumb cat ran across the street and got run over and it serves him right. Because I love from the inside out I'm cool and in control and it doesn't bother me."

It was quite normal and appropriate for her to be angry and upset and to shed some tears—but not to still be shedding them six months later.

What is inappropriate is to keep the hurt alive. To allow anger to fester into resentment and bitterness. To allow those unhappy experiences of the past to control my life today, to keep me from growing and changing. I have a choice, and my choice is to cling to harsh feelings and blame others or to acknowledge the past and move on.

Communicate Your Feelings

One way to handle our hurt feelings is to learn to communicate them to others in a wholesome way. Basically there are two kinds of messages we give when we express our feelings. The first is the "you" message, which is aggressive.

An aggressive message involves using feelings in a punitive way. It is hitting the other person with words. It invites defensiveness and retaliation. Here are some aggressive messages: "You don't care for me." "You never listen. No wonder I can't communicate with you." "You have a foul mouth."

What do you see about these kinds of statements? They all involve blame and accusation. They close down communication and invite quarreling. How can we turn these aggressive, punitive statements around so we can express the truth about our feelings without punishing others or making them responsible for our attitudes? I believe the best way is to learn to express ourselves through the second kind of message: the assertive message.

An assertive message keeps communication open because it invites reflection and consideration. Let's look at the same messages we read previously, but turn them into assertive statements.

"I'm feeling uncared for." Notice there is no blame and no accusation. I am simply being honest with my feelings.

"I can't seem to get my point across to you, and I'm feeling frustrated." Those are facts. No one can debate them. Because it's not an accusation, the other person will not become defensive.

"You have a foul mouth" becomes "I really feel uncomfortable when you use those words."

Most of us would be able to communicate our feelings—especially the negative ones—more effectively and positively if we would learn to give assertive messages rather than aggressive ones.

It's a matter of responding to people rather than reacting to them. When we react, they control our lives. When we respond to people, we are acting responsibly.

In his book *Why Am I Afraid to Tell You Who I Am?* John Powell relates a story he attributes to the syndicated columnist Sydney Harris. Harris tells of accompanying his friend to a newsstand. The friend greeted the newsman very courteously, but in return received gruff and discourteous service. Accepting the newspaper which was shoved rudely in his direction, Harris' friend politely smiled and wished the newsman a nice weekend. As the two friends walked down the street, the columnist asked, "Does he always treat you so rudely?"

"Yes, unfortunately he does."

"And are you always so polite and friendly to him?"

"Yes, I am."

"Why are you so nice to him when he is so unfriendly to you?"

"Because I don't want *him* to decide how *I'm* going to act."

I WILL LET
NO ONE DECIDE
MY DAY

If I react to someone's vulgarity and crudeness, I'm playing their game—I'm dancing on the end of their string. I've allowed their problem to become my problem. But if I respond to their vulgarity and crudeness from the graciousness of my circle, it's still their problem. I don't want to let them decide how I'm going to live. Who's running your life? Anyone you react to.

I heard a story the other day about a grandfather who was walking down the streets of the city with his grandson. On the sidewalk they passed a woman reputed to be the town prostitute. The grandfather graciously doffed his hat to the woman as they passed by.

The young boy said, "Why'd you do that to that kind of woman?"

The old grandfather replied, "I don't know what kind of woman she is. All I know is that *I am a gentleman.*"

You see, it doesn't matter who you pass on the street. It doesn't matter what kind of people you work with. It doesn't really matter who you're married to. That's not the issue. The issue is, who you are. That's what really matters. But, if I don't like who I am, what am I going to do? I'm going to blame somebody out there and try to hold them responsible.

We are all self-made people. Only the successful will admit it.

Outwitted
He drew a circle that shut me out—
Heretic, rebel, a thing to flout.
But Love and I had the wit to win:
We drew a circle that took him in.
EDWIN MARKHAM

Step Five to Becoming a Great Lover: I accept full responsibility for everything I think, feel, say, and choose.

Workshop:

1. Go to the Values Inventory and check how you answered question 7, "Are you fun to live with, why or why not?" Whether your answer was yes or no, did you accept responsibility for your answer, especially a "no" answer? Also, check question 16, "How did you get where you are?" Was your answer choice or chance? Also, pay special attention to how you answered questions 8, 26, 29, 35, and 37 on the Self-Esteem Exercise.

2. Change the following aggressive statements into assertive messages:
   Aggressive: "You really make me mad."
   Assertive: "_____"
   Aggressive: "You make me so frustrated."
   Assertive: "_____"
   Aggressive: "You really did embarrass me last night."
   Assertive: "_____"

3. Change the following statements into sentences reflecting a responsible willingness to live from the inside out.
   "George made me do it." _____
   "School was boring."_____
   "Stupid golf clubs!" _____

4. Identify anything or anybody that you have been holding responsible for holding you back and make a conscious decision right now to stop blaming.

6

You Are What You Think You Are

"I can't help it! It's just the way I am!"

How often have you heard someone say these words? Perhaps you've said them yourself once in a while. There is an element of truth to "I can't help it." Yet, I wonder how someone who believes that would respond to the question, "Do you *want* to be different?"

More often than not, I suspect the response will be, "Not really." But we *can* change ourselves. It's a matter of desire. It's not just a question of who we are, but who we are becoming.

Yet most of us are threatened by change. We have a "comfort zone," and it's difficult to move out of it. In fact, we seldom will move out until something "discomforts" us enough to outweigh the comfort of staying where we are. Growth does not take place without overcoming problems. We are all lazy at heart; we will not grow unless we have to in order to survive. We also tend to dig in if we sense that another person is trying to change us.

There are two reasons why we dig in, stubbornly clinging to our ways. The first is our fear that we are unacceptable the way we are—which causes us to be defensive. The second is our fear that the other person is controlling us—which prompts us to be stubborn.

Yet to be in a healthy place, we need to be able to accept ourselves *as we are* and at the same time realize that we have a lot of growing to do. Growing doesn't seem as threatening to us as changing. But, of course, if we're growing, we're changing. There is no status quo. We are always in process.

There are two basic views about "who we are." The first is: "Eighty percent of my personality was formed by the time I was five or six years old. I've been around quite a few years, and I'm pretty set in my ways. You can't teach an old dog new tricks. That's just the way I am—yesterday, today, and forever. I just can't help it." And, to a limited degree, it's true, but it's also a cop-out.

The second attitude is to say, "I don't know what happened to me in those early years, but it obviously wasn't totally devastating. I've got quite a few years left which means quite a few choices left, which means I can choose what I want to be. As of today, I choose to accept full responsibility for who I am, and I will grow to be the person I want to be."

We are profoundly influenced by others very early in life, but we must remember and insist that we are free and responsible for what we will become. If we are willing to act against inhibiting or crippling feelings, we will be able to change our habits of behavior and consequently the course of our lives!

My guess is that you have already chosen the second option or you wouldn't even be reading this book.

I think it's obvious that the longer a person waits to make the change, the more difficult it will be. But it is *never* impossible. How, then, do we make changes in ourselves? How did we come to be who we are in the first place? It is true that both our genetic heritage and our environment have something to do with who we are. But, primarily, we are the sum total of the thoughts, images, and experiences we've been storing in our minds from the day we were born.

Understanding Your Mind

In a sense, all three of these are really the same. In other words, we don't think in words, we think in pictures or images. For instance, if I were lecturing to you and I said the word *house,* you wouldn't see the word *house.* In your imagination you would see a picture of a house. It might be ranch-style, or two-story, or brick, or colonial, but it would be a picture.

Similarly, if I were to mention camping to you, your mind would take you to a favored spot in the woods or the desert or the beach—wherever you have been camping or wherever you have seen campers in pictures.

The odds are, you may have "experienced" something like falling off a cliff, only to awaken in a cold sweat safely on the edge of your own bed. Your heart was pounding, but nothing had really happened. Your mind was only "picturing." Your subconscious mind—your nervous system—doesn't know the difference between what really happens and what you imagine (picture) happens. It accepts every experience *as if* it were real.

To help us understand how the subconscious mind works, let's take a nontechnical look at the relationship between it and the conscious mind. Figure 2 is a simple illustration of the human mind.

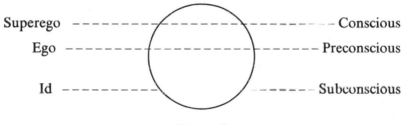

Figure 2.

The mind is made up of three parts—the conscious (or superego), the preconscious (or ego), and the subconscious (or id). These three aspects of the mind are constantly interacting, and consequently the mind is a composite of thoughts, images, and experiences on the three levels.

The top (or surface) part of the mind shown in Figure 2 is the superego, or the conscious. In transactional analysis, it is referred to as the *parent*. It is the area of our minds in which we see, feel, and are aware. In the conscious, we reason, make decisions, and exercise our free will. We make judgments and determine likes and dislikes in our conscious minds. Consciously, we remember the events of the past.

This conscious—or *parent*—part of our mind is somewhat of a legislative–judicial branch of our mental government. It makes and enforces the rules and regulations. From the conscious part of our minds we discipline ourselves and work toward security. It contains our conscience and our ideals. It is here that we experience guilt when our conscience is violated and shame when we fail to meet our ideals.

The preconscious area, also known as the ego, includes those things of which we are not at this moment conscious, but which we could make conscious with little difficulty. For example, at this moment you are only vaguely aware of a number of circumstances that are immediately affecting you, because your awareness of them is at a preconscious level. You are not thinking about them as you concentrate on this page.

Now, let me make you aware of some preconscious feelings. Stop for a moment and determine whether you feel cold or warm. Whether the texture of this book's cover is rough or smooth. Whether the chair you are sitting in is soft and cozy, or straight and firm. You are now thinking of several things that have been a part of your preconscious cognizance, but of which you were not actively aware until I brought them to your conscious mind.

This preconscious or *adult* part of our minds serves as the executive branch of our mental government. Its major function is to keep the peace—and balance—between the conscious and the subconscious mind. Most of us do not have strong enough egos to maintain constant balance, and so we swing between the two extremes. (See the chart, Figure 3.)

A mature ego allows flexibility between the new and the old, between work and play, between risk taking and caution. An immature ego is not flexible. To be "safe" it usually locks in on one extreme or the other. And this, of course, prevents growth.

Balance, Congruence, Flexibility—The Task of the Ego

ID	**EGO**	**SUPEREGO**
(*Child*)	(*Adult*)	(*Parent*)

New ----------------------------Old

Play---------------------------Work

Freedom ------------------------Discipline

Liberal ------------------------Conservative

Progressive ---------------------Secure

Takes risks ----- --------------Plays it safe

Gives a little extra ------------------Pays minimum wage

A cheerful giver ---------------------A strict tither

Sensual problems -----------------Attitudinal problems

If you eliminate the *parent*, you are <u>irresponsible.</u>

If you eliminate the *child*, you are <u>bored.</u>

A healthy, mature, congruent, spiritual ego . . .

Keeps freedom from becoming license, anarchy, irresponsibility.

Keeps security from becoming a prison, or apathetic, or careless.

It's not either/or, but *both*.

GO FOR IT ----------- with ----------- Good judgment

Boundless freedom ------ with ----------- Order

Figure 3.

By far, the greatest part of our mental activity takes place in the subconscious. The subconscious is like a vast storehouse—the Library of Congress in our mental government, so to speak. From our first breath—and probably even prenatally, *everything* that has entered our minds through our five senses is stored there—*forever.* It is this vast storehouse that most profoundly affects the way we live our daily lives.

From this subconscious storehouse, which has no awareness of time, we are motivated to take risks, to play, to operate from feelings rather than facts. We also dream, have nightmares, and sometimes make choices that surprise or alarm us on the conscious level.

Most of us have asked ourselves questions like, *I wonder why I did that? Why can't I do what I want to? Why is it the harder I try, the worse it gets?*

These kinds of questions are indicative of the kind of struggle that goes on between the conscious and subconscious parts of our minds. We are all aware of inner conflicts that we find difficult to understand. And the more intense and unresolved the conflict, the more we experience dis-ease.

Perhaps you've heard somebody say, "I'm free to do as I please." Others might say, "Man is given free will." These statements are only partially true because:

THE ONLY FREEDOM WE HAVE
IS THE ABILITY TO CHOOSE
THAT TO WHICH WE WILL BE
SLAVES

I am free to choose (consciously) what I put or allow into my subconscious mind. But once it is there, my free will is over. By that I mean that approximately 90 percent of what we do is habit. We don't think about it. Most of what we do is out of habit, and in that sense we are slaves to our subconscious minds. That may be good or bad—depending upon what we have been allowing in the subconscious.

We couldn't function if the subconscious mind didn't take care of us. If we had to *think* about everything we do all day we would probably blow our fuses. So, most of what we do is from habit. In a sense, we *practice* the thoughts, images, and experiences we put into our subconscious minds.

We either have positive thoughts, or we have negative thoughts. I think the words *positive* and *negative* have lost a lot of their impact because of overuse, and because of that, people are rather indifferent to them. Let me suggest a couple of fresher words that might give more meaning.

To the word negative, let's add the words *destructive* and *poisonous.* To the word *positive,* let's add the words *creative* and *nourishing.* Our positive, creative, nourishing thoughts, images, and experiences promote growth and life. Our negative, destructive, poisonous thoughts, images, and experiences lead to death. And who controls that? **We do.** Each of us is responsible for our own mental input. A great lover is responsible for his own thoughts, his own feelings, his own attitudes.

Here's the process and our choice: We are either putting into our minds positive, creative, and nourishing thoughts that cause us to grow and live, or we are allowing negative, destructive, and toxic thoughts that harm us.

Let's say, for example, that every night before I go to bed I read murder mystery stories. I willingly choose to fill my subconscious mind with the contents of murder mysteries. After several nights of this, as might be expected, I experience nightmares. The next day I run into you at the office and I tell you, "Man, did I have some terrible dreams last night, but I guess I can't help what I dream."

Can I help what I dream? The answer to that is no. I cannot help what I dream. When my conscious mind is shut down in sleep, the subconscious acts freely. But the answer also has to be yes, because I am responsible for what I put into my subconscious. It should be obvious that if I do not wish to have nightmares, I might choose to read something different before I go to sleep.

I know of a housewife who watches soap operas all day long

and wonders why she is depressed and in a bad mood when her
husband comes home. I'd be in a bad mood, too, if I were carrying the burden of the world on my shoulders, as it turns on the
edge of night, waiting for the guiding light to lead me in search
for tomorrow among the young and the restless. No one can take
in all that nonloving data and not have it affect them.

When a person listens to it and listens to it and listens to it, she
becomes emotionally involved. One day her husband comes
home, makes a simple remark, and she says to herself, *Oh, no!
That's exactly what Adam said to Cecily before he divorced
her on "The Young Lion Tamers." It must be all over for me!* It's
déjà vu.

Soap opera fans are famous for confusing fact with fiction
when one of their loved ones is done in on the tube. So what happens when the victim is a psychiatrist to whom millions of viewers
feel intimately attached? Pandemonium.

In a recent episode of "Days of Our Lives" Marlena Evans, one
of the show's main characters, was murdered by the Salem Stran-
gler. Within minutes of the murder thousands of viewers around
the country were distraught enough to phone NBC headquarters
in Burbank, California. Hundreds of people in Los Angeles were
angry enough to picket the studio. And actress Deidre Hall, who
plays the part of Dr. Evans, spent a day and a half logging tearful
outbursts from fans who were convinced she had succumbed. As
it turned out, the doctor had not been murdered. It was simply an
elaborate ruse of mistaken identity to manipulate the vulnerable
fans.

Recent statistics show that television sets in American homes
are on an average of 6.5 hours per day. Television is absorbing
14,000 valuable hours during the course of childhood. That is
equivalent to sitting before the tube 8 hours a day, continuously
for 4.9 years. That's hard for me to fathom. What an impact that
must make on the lives of our children. By the time they're grown
they'll have spent more time in front of the television set than in
school or than they've spent with their parents. And we wonder

why they seem to live by somebody else's philosophy of life and code of ethics.

Television is one of the most important learning tools we have, but it is so easy to become indiscriminate in our watching. Reports indicate that by the time the average child becomes fourteen years of age, he will have witnessed nearly eighteen thousand murders on television. This past season, for example, we were offered hilariously "funny" episodes involving abortion, divorce, extramarital relationships, rape, and the ever-popular theme: "Father is an idiot." In the name of "social relevance" the foundations of the family and all that represents the Christian ethic are being hacked away.

With that kind of exposure, what will children begin to accept as the norm? If you really get upset with someone, are you supposed to sit down and talk it out? Heck, no! Blow 'em away! But then, it can't be all that serious—when the guy who gets blown away shows up in the next episode.

"But that isn't logical!" someone might say. "Actors aren't portraying reality—it's only pretend. We know it's not real." That's true—on the conscious level. The problem is, the subconscious mind believes it *is* real. The subconscious mind does not think; it does not argue; it does not evaluate; it does not make any judgments. Whatever we tell our subconscious mind, it believes.

Getting in Touch With Your Subconscious

One way to get in touch with what is in our subconscious is to take the following exercise. This exercise will bring to the surface some important attitudes about ourselves.

Simply write the very first thought that comes to your mind, even if the sentence doesn't make perfect sense to you. Do not skip any questions, and don't try to write "good" answers or "right" answers or the kind of answers you think you "should" write, because that will invalidate the exercise.

Complete the following sentences:

1. When the odds are against me, _____
2. If I were in charge, _____
3. To me, the future looks _____
4. The people over me _____
5. I am afraid of _____
6. I feel that a real friend _____
7. My idea of a perfect person is _____
8. Compared with most families, mine _____
9. I believe I have the ability to _____
10. People don't know I feel _____
11. My family treats me like _____
12. I don't like people who _____
13. My greatest mistake was _____
14. I wish my spouse _____
15. My greatest weakness is _____
16. My dream is _____
17. The people I like best _____
18. I like working with people who _____
19. My sex life _____
20. What I want most out of life _____
21. People whom I consider my superiors _____
22. God is _____
23. People who work with me _____
24. I could be perfectly happy if _____
25. It seems to me I am best in _____
26. The thing that really upsets me is _____
27. Someday, I will _____
28. If I had more money _____
29. The disease that concerns me is _____
30. My most valuable possession _____

Look back over your list. Try to imagine how you would react if a perfect stranger said those same things about you. Would you feel good, or would you feel hurt? Would you be indignant?

Have you ever tripped over something and called yourself

clumsy? Have you ever made an error in your checkbook and called yourself dumb, or incompetent, or stupid? Have you ever been in an uncomfortable or embarrassing situation and called yourself a fool? If you have, you have been talking to yourself in a way you would never address someone you love. Why do you do that?

Perhaps you don't love yourself or hold yourself in very high esteem. Maybe you think you're just making light of a situation—that you're poking some good-natured fun at yourself. Unfortunately, your subconscious mind doesn't know you're kidding. It believes what you tell it. It doesn't evaluate or make judgments as to whether the information is true or false. Just like a computer, it accepts whatever you feed it.

THE MOST POWERFUL FORCE I HAVE
IS WHAT I SAY TO MYSELF AND BELIEVE

All of our lives we have been collecting these nourishing or destructive thoughts and feelings in our minds. Whatever is in there is in there forever; we cannot get it out. If most of what's in our minds is negative, and I've just told you we can't get it out, that could prove very discouraging. At best it would let us off the hook from the standpoint of responsibility, and we could say, "See, I told you I couldn't help it."

But I want to suggest a marvelous concept that we can use to change our lives. The key word is *dilution.* We cannot remove what is in our subconscious mind, but we *can* dilute it.

To help us understand this concept, let's think of the mind as a swimming pool. Twice a week you will put chlorine and acid— poison—into the water. After about a fifteen-minute wait, you can dive in and swim unafraid of all that poison because it is diluted.

What if the chlorine and acid were all out of balance, and there was little or no water in the pool? You wouldn't dare swim because the chlorine would literally burn your eyes, and the acid would eat your skin. To make matters worse, you cannot get the poison out. The solution is to add fresh water daily until the balance is restored and it's safe.

But there is a problem. What happens if you add fresh water every morning—and more poison every night? The dilution won't work. Many people think that attending a personal development seminar or reading a book will change their lives, but old habits die hard.

If we really want to change our habits, we must change the input that feeds them. The cycle must be broken—and it can be.

Most of us are familiar with the letters GIGO, which stand for Garbage In—Garbage Out. It's a phrase commonly used among computer people, and it means that the computer is no better than the information it is fed. What you get out of it is determined by what you put into it. And so it is with our minds. Instead of continuing to put in the garbage, we're going to learn to practice recycling it.

Every waking moment we talk to ourselves about the things we experience. Our self-talk, the thoughts that we communicate to ourselves, in turn controls the way we feel and act. In the next chapter I am going to discuss how we can use the power of self-talk creatively in order to grow, in order to change our lives, in order to make love a habit.

Step Six to Becoming a Great Lover: I prefer to allow only creative and nourishing thoughts and images to enter my mind. I can, however, learn and grow from *all* experiences.

Workshop:

1. Check back to the Values Inventory to question 4, "What do you like best about yourself?" and 6, "List some of the fears

you are aware of." This will give you an insight to some of your self-talk.

2. Review your "Complete the Sentence" exercise. Put a + mark in front of each "positive" response and a − mark in front of each "negative" response. What does this observation tell you about yourself? Does it give you anything to work on?
3. How does a healthy ego help keep our lives stable?
4. Why do we resist change?

7

Making Love a Habit

Did you ever stop to think of the impact that words have on our lives? We look to words for comfort, for strength, for courage. Words draw men into battle and words pave the way for peace. They offer assurance of survival and they threaten our sense of security.

Words stir our spirits or plunge us into the depths of despair. They offer us insights and enable us to communicate with one another, while they stimulate our emotions and challenge our beliefs. They can be loyal servants or cruel taskmasters.

Words often influence us, even when we're unaware of it. To see how this can happen, slowly read the following lists aloud. Think about how you feel as you pronounce each term:

Critical	Ugly	Moody
Clumsy	Tired	Damned
Bored	Afraid	Listless
Sick	Mean	Thoughtless
Stingy	Hateful	Grudging
Rotten	Sloppy	Uptight

How do these words make you feel? Do you feel up? Are you excited? Can you go out and win the world? Probably not. Now consider these words that are opposites of those you just read. Try to be in touch with your feelings as you slowly say each of the following words aloud:

Appreciative	Enthusiastic	Kind
Lovely	Blessed	Cheerful
Courteous	Eager	Fearless
Forgiving	Growing	Harmonious
Healthy	Loving	Generous
Relaxed	Unselfish	Thoughtful

How do these expressions affect you? As you read the lists, did the tone of your voice change? We need to be aware of the impact of words and thoughts on our lives, because, in a very real sense, they make us what we are. There is no such thing as an unimportant word or an unimportant sentence. Every word we speak has an emotional impact.

Dehumanizing Each Other

Equally important is what we say to others. Our words feed *their* subconscious minds with messages, too. One of the biggest problems we face in our relationships is our tendency to use harmful labels that can affect the self-esteem of others.

Labels cause all kinds of problems for us because we tend to live up to the names we (or others) call ourselves. We perform according to how we see ourselves; and others perform according to how they see themselves in our eyes.

It was primarily because of this labeling process that I developed my Affirmation Cards. The sayings from my cards are seen throughout this book. One day I was aware that I had seen the same poster in offices all across the United States. The poster read: IT'S DIFFICULT TO SOAR WITH EAGLES WHEN YOU WORK WITH TURKEYS. The message is, "How can you expect me to succeed in a world full of 'turkeys'?" This is how the poster should read, but I don't think you could get anyone to hang it on their wall: IT'S IMPOSSIBLE TO SOAR WITH EAGLES IF YOU PERCEIVE YOURSELF AS A TURKEY.

People are not turkeys—or ding-a-lings—or flakes; they are human beings just like we are. We dehumanize in order to justify our failure to relate.

Why do we call people names and make judgments on them? Out of our sense of inadequacy we use negative labels to rationalize our inability to relate to others.

Some time ago I held a seminar for a police department. The men spent half the morning debating the definition of a human being. They kept using harsh words like *inhuman, garbage, vermin, rat.* I was astonished and puzzled by the debate. Suddenly it dawned on me what the problem was: You can't shoot *human beings.*

Out of that experience, I developed a theory: One human being *cannot* destroy another human being. Man's inhumanity to man is rampant—but before we can destroy another life, we must first dehumanize the other person.

In war, for example, we convince soldiers that everybody on the other side of the battle is a rat. We can shoot rats all day and sleep well at night, but we cannot handle the emotional trauma of destroying another person.

What is the whole debate about abortion? It's the same debate the policemen had: What is human? If an unborn child is a *human being* and we destroy it, we will suffer the pangs of guilt and grief. So, we must rationalize. We must dehumanize and refer to it as a "fetus" or an "embryo," or, better yet, just "tissue." If you want it, it's a *baby.* If you don't want it, it's a *thing.*

The problem is, rationalizing doesn't change a thing. No matter how much rationalizing we do, we have destroyed. We all dehumanize others sometime.

The most common way we dehumanize is with words. *Phony. Slob. Turkey. Pig. Brat. Stupid. Klutz. Flake.* If you're not human, I don't have to deal with you.

In thousands of cases, divorce has had a terrible history of dehumanizing. In the process of severing the relationship, you hear things like, "I don't know what I ever saw in that woman; she turned out to be 'no good,' a real 'loser.' " And with those kinds of dehumanizing labels, you can probably get some sympathy. "I wouldn't want to live with something like that, either!" It doesn't make any sense to walk away from a wonderful, warm, understanding *human being*. It's easy to walk away from a "no-good bum."

Destructive words and phrases wrap themselves around us and our friends and families like strands of a spider's thread. We're scarcely aware of how damaging and negative they are, and consequently we offer them little attention until they multiply into webs that will not let us go.

In the last chapter I mentioned the affirmation,

THE MOST POWERFUL FORCE
WE POSSESS IS WHAT WE SAY
TO OURSELVES AND BELIEVE

This force is powerful in the lives of others, too. To be great lovers, we must seek to use that power creatively. But before we can help others be creative, we must first be creative ourselves.

Control Your Self-Talk

Many of our thoughts are destructive, but we do not recognize them as such. We have to train ourselves to transform our harmful self-talk into nourishing self-talk. All of our senses are so bombarded by negative media that unless we make a conscious effort to control what we allow to enter our subconscious minds, we will simply lose the battle by default.

In order to get a handle on what you are saying to yourself, try this brief exercise. Take a blank sheet of paper and fold it down the middle with the open edge to the left. Then take the next few moments to write on the front of the paper all the negative thoughts, feelings, and attitudes you have about yourself.

Think of these negatives in terms of the roles you play—parent, child, sibling, friend, student, employee, employer, husband, wife. No one will see this list, so you can feel free to write honestly. If you have trouble getting started, perhaps some of the following statements will help you:

- I take things too seriously
- I yell at my children too much
- I'm too lazy
- I'm always late
- I'm too shy
- I'm too fat
- I can't be trusted
- I hold grudges
- I'm a drunk
- I never have time to do what I want
- I can't seem to get out of debt
- I'm critical

Write as many statements as you can, as long as you believe they are true of yourself. If you can't seem to think of anything to write, start with "I'm afraid to be honest," because that is probably what is holding you back.

Then turn the paper over to the other side, so the open edge is to the right. On this side of the paper list the qualities of the kind of person you would really like to be, if you had no fears, no anxieties, nothing to hold you back. If you had the *power* and *authority* to declare the kind of person you would like to be, what would you *be?* (Not what would you like to *do.*)

Do not permit humility to get in your way, and do not allow realism to hinder you. Be idealistic. If you have trouble getting started, turn to the end of this chapter and choose some of the words on the Being Words List or the 100 Words for a More Positive, Creative Vocabulary. Fill your paper, describing the person you would truly like to be.

When you have finished, open the paper and look at both sides of the page. Compare the two lists you have written. As you study the two sides, do you see any relationship between them? Are there parallels? Are there opposites?

Sometimes people will notice a difference in their own handwriting. The list on the left—the negatives—will frequently be written in smaller, tighter script. Often the penmanship is careless. The list on the right—the positives—will reveal larger, more open penmanship and will seem to flow more freely.

In your daily life, which of the two lists do you tend to think about more often? For most people, it is the left side—the negatives. If this is true of you, then the qualities and characteristics you listed there probably dominate your personality because those are the thoughts that you dwell on.

Assuming you would like to become the person on the right side of the paper, what would it take? It's a matter of *giving those qualities and characteristics the same focus and attention you have been giving to the left side.* **AS A MAN THINKETH—SO HE IS!** The solution is simple, but it is not easy to accomplish because changing a habit is such a difficult task that it becomes mental warfare.

There are three basic steps in changing the negative self-talk habit to a love habit. The first is to *refuse to be enslaved* to the items on the negative list. The only freedom we have is the ability to choose what will control us. Once a destructive thought is in our subconscious, we submit to it until we choose to change it, dilute it, or recycle it.

What happens when a negative thought emerges from your subconscious mind? What should you do with that thought? If you are like most people, you consider it, worry about it, cultivate it, and reinforce it. Driving it back and forth, you unintentionally make it stronger than it was originally.

What if I were to ask you to stand in a corner of the room for thirty minutes, and, during that time, you were *not* to think of pink elephants. You would spend thirty minutes trying to think of ways *not* to think of pink elephants. The harder you tried, the worse it would be. There is only one way to avoid thinking about pink elephants, and that is to think deliberately and consciously *about something else.*

That is precisely how we can make the change from negative,

destructive thinking to positive, creative thinking. It is not a matter of stopping the fear, but of learning to love. Not getting rid of the darkness, but turning on the light. Not ridding ourselves of the left side of the paper, but focusing on the right side and making *it* the reality.

The second step toward making love a habit is to *recycle those destructive thoughts.* Recycling the garbage involves the use of a simple formula to translate the destructive statement into a creative, nourishing one.

For example, perhaps one of the statements on my negative list is, "I talk too much." To recycle this statement, this is the process:

Personal I
Present tense . . . am
Positive . . . . . attentive

Here are some other examples:

Negatives	**I**	**am**	**Positive Statement**
Procrastinator	I	am	decisive.
Impatient	I	am	patient.
Easily manipulated	I	am	purposeful.
Greedy	I	am	generous.
Critical	I	am	understanding.
Too shy	I	am	outgoing and interested in others.

Now look again at the list of negatives you wrote. On a separate piece of paper, rewrite it so that all of the statements follow the formula. Each statement will begin with "I am." Remember, it is not "I will" or "I should" or "I can" or "I'm going to." We are talking about *being,* not *doing.* It's not a question of what you would like to *do,* but what kind of person you would like to *be.* Remember that being comes before doing. If you have trouble turning your statements around, you might want to refer to the Being Words List at the end of this chapter.

After you write your own list, there are two ways it can be

helpful to you. First, you can wait until a negative thought surfaces and then block the thought immediately by recycling it with the "I am" statement. The second and better method is to begin to flood (dilute) your subconscious mind with everything on your "I am" list before the negative thought ever gets a chance to surface in the first place. In other words, begin to say to yourself, *I am attentive. I am generous. I am considerate.*

"Wait a minute!" you might be saying. "I can't say those things to myself. They aren't true. They're lies. I'm not attentive or considerate or generous!"

It may be true that you don't see yourself that way, but what makes you think everything on your negative list is true? Remember, the most powerful force that we possess may be what we say to ourselves *and believe.* The *and believe* part is a bonus. Our subconscious mind accepts whatever we feed it. If we *believe* what we say, it's *twice* as powerful, but you don't have to believe it for it to work. Which statements are true for you? Whichever you *choose* to believe!

I want you to notice another profound truth about your list. Every phrase on the negative side could be summed up with "I am fearful." Every phrase on the positive side of the page could be "I am loving." Do you remember how we get rid of our fear? By focusing on the love! If you will begin right now to focus and concentrate on the love phrases on the right-hand page, they will eventually replace all the fear phrases on the left-hand page.

I HAVE THE POWER TO
DECLARE
THE PERSON I AM BECOMING

I'd like to suggest that you add two additional "I am's" to your list if they are not already there. The first one is "I am grateful." No matter how I look, no matter what I know, no matter what I do, no matter what I have, I am grateful. That means I recognize that a lot of what I am and what I have has been given to me. We are all gifted.

Second, add "I am human." That will let you blow it. Permit you to make mistakes. Allow you to get away from perfectionism. Set you free to grow and change.

The third step in learning how to make love a habit is to *repeat the positives.* Everything we've ever learned has been by repetition, practice, rehearsal. Did you ever learn to play a musical instrument? If so, you practiced again and again until you mastered the music. You consciously fed your subconscious until you were able to do it automatically.

No matter what we try to learn, our goal is to be able to use our knowledge or skill without having to think about it. Did you ever notice that many people can type unconsciously until they come to a number? It's because the numbers are used so rarely that few of us master them on the keyboard.

Most professional basketball players have probably been dribbling a basketball since the day they could walk. (The current greatest seasonal hockey scorer, Wayne Gretzke, started on skates when he was two years old.) As a result, they can dribble a basketball about as naturally as they walk. They run up and down the court without giving dribbling a thought. Their minds are free to think of strategy, because dribbling is second nature to them. They are free to play basketball because of hundreds of hours of disciplined practice. It's a paradox. *The only freedom is in discipline.*

To get an idea as to how this paradox works, listen to the phrases commonly used to describe an athlete at his best: "He's out of his mind." "He's playing over his head." "He's unconscious." "He doesn't know what he's doing." The common factor in each of these descriptions is what might be called "mindlessness." They know that their peak performances never come when they're *thinking* about it.

Clearly, to play unconsciously does not mean to play without consciousness. That would be quite difficult! It means the athlete is playing without giving himself a lot of instructions on how to hit the ball, or how to correct past mistakes, or how to repeat what he just did. He is conscious, but not thinking. If an athlete is on a "hot streak" it usually continues until he starts thinking about it and tries to maintain it; as soon as he attempts to exercise control, he loses it.

Being Consciously Unconscious

Can a person learn to play or live "out of their mind" on purpose? How can you be consciously unconscious? It sounds like a contradiction in terms, but it can be achieved. It's called *concentration.* The mind is so focused that it is still. It becomes one with what the body is doing, and the unconscious or automatic functions are working without interference from thoughts. The *concentrated* mind has no room for thinking of the how-to's of doing. (For more information on this subject, you can read *The Inner Game,* by W. Timothy Gallwey.)

The power of how we practice in our imagination was dramatically illustrated by an experiment reported in Maxwell Maltz's book, *Psycho-Cybernetics:*[1]

> *Research Quarterly* reported an experiment on the effects of mental practice on improving skill in sinking basketball free throws. One group of students actually practiced throwing the ball every day for 20 days, and were scored on the first and last days.
>
> A second group was scored on the first and last days, and engaged in no sort of practice in between.
>
> A third group was scored on the first day, then spent 20 minutes a day imagining that they were throwing the ball at the goal. When they missed, they would imagine that they corrected their aim accordingly.
>
> The first group, which actually practiced 20 minutes every day, improved in scoring *24 per cent.*

1. PSYCHO-CYBERNETICS by Maxwell Maltz, M.D., F.I.C.S. Copyright © 1960 by Prentice-Hall, Inc. Published by Prentice-Hall, Inc., Englewood Cliffs, New Jersey 07632.

The second group, which had no sort of practice, showed no improvement.

The third group, which practiced in their imagination, improved in scoring *23 per cent!*

Just *one* percentage point difference!

Do you remember that I mentioned at the beginning of chapter 6 that the subconscious mind doesn't know the difference between what is real and what is imagined? So, what are we doing all day in our mind? We're practicing. What are we practicing? Losing or winning? Succeeding or failing? Making it or not making it? Being accepted or being rejected? Forgiveness or resentment? We must not underestimate the power of our imagination. All of what we are today is the result of what we have been practicing.

To become great lovers, we must practice what loving is all about. To paraphrase Goethe: If I practice what I am, I will remain what I am. If I practice what I would like to be, that is what I will become.

One way to practice is to read our "I am" lists and our 100 Words For a More Positive, Creative Vocabulary to ourselves regularly. The best time to read them is at night before retiring and again first thing in the morning.

Another way to practice putting these creative, nourishing thoughts into our minds is to record both lists onto a cassette and then to play the tape while doing other things. Let it play while we drive, while we soak in the bathtub, while we work in the garden, or tinker in the garage. As the material saturates our minds over a period of time, it will make a difference.

It is never too late to change. We cannot go back and start over, but we do have today. We can be free of our negative self-images, we can be free to love others. We can be free to become successful, happy people if we discipline our thoughts. What we do now can make us what we want to be tomorrow. We can make love a habit.

I HAVE THE COURAGE
TO EMBRACE THE
GREATNESS
FOR WHICH I WAS BORN

Step Seven to Becoming a Great Lover: I will treat people *as if* they were what they could be—including *myself!*

Workshop:

1. Complete your list of positive, creative words that you want to add to your vocabulary. Go over the list daily for at least thirty days.
2. Without delay, recycle all of your negative thoughts into positive thoughts, so you will be ready the next time that negative thought surfaces. Complete your "I Am" list.
3. What is the dilution process and how does it work?
4. What is the three-step formula for recycling?
5. Why do we dehumanize people?
6. List some dehumanizing words that you have been using that you would like to eliminate:_____

   _____
7. What is the paradox of freedom?
8. What is the "secret" for becoming what we want to be?

"I Am" List
BEING WORDS

I AM HEALTHY
I AM HOPEFUL
I AM OPTIMISTIC
I AM FUN-LOVING
I AM VIGOROUS
I AM ENERGETIC
I AM SATISFIED
I AM RELAXED
I AM FRIENDLY
I AM CARING
I AM LOVING
I AM TRUSTING
I AM THOUGHTFUL
I AM TENDER
I AM ACCEPTED
I AM ADMIRED
I AM COURTEOUS
I AM RESPONSIBLE
I AM SELF-CONTROLLED
I AM COOPERATIVE
I AM PARTICIPATIVE
I AM INFLUENTIAL
I AM PERSUASIVE
I AM AWARE
I AM INFORMED
I AM ALERT

I AM SENSITIVE
I AM OPEN-MINDED
I AM WISE
I AM PURPOSEFUL
I AM RATIONAL
I AM EMPATHETIC
I AM UNDERSTANDING
I AM COMPETENT
I AM PROFICIENT
I AM RESOURCEFUL
I AM MASTERFUL
I AM ABLE
I AM CAPABLE
I AM CREATIVE
I AM HELPFUL
I AM GENEROUS
I AM LOVABLE
I AM ETHICAL
I AM LOYAL
I AM CONSIDERATE
I AM HUMANE
I AM GENUINE
I AM TRUSTWORTHY
I AM CONCERNED
  ABOUT OTHERS

100 Words For A More Positive, Creative Vocabulary

Ability
Abundance
Admiration
Adoration
Affection
Amazement
Appreciation
Balance
Beauty
Blessing
Bravery
Calmness
Caring
Cheerfulness
Childlikeness
Commitment
Compassion
Confidence
Consideration
Courage
Courtesy
Creativity
Decisiveness
Dedication
Delight
Dependability
Devotion
Dignity
Discipline
Eagerness
Elegance
Empathy
Enjoyment

Enthusiasm
Esteem
Excellence
Faithfulness
Fearlessness
Forgiveness
Friendliness
Giving
Grace
Gratitude
Growing
Happiness
Harmony
Health
Honorable
Hope
Joy
Kindness
Laughter
Leadership
Listening
Love
Magnificence
Majesty
Optimism
Order
Peacefulness
Persistence
Politeness
Positiveness
Praise
Process
Productivity

Purposefulness
Relaxation
Resourcefulness
Respect
Responsible
Responsiveness
Reverence
Sacredness
Sensitive
Serenity
Service
Simplicity
Spontaneousness
Stability
Success
Tenderhearted
Tenderness
Thanksgiving
Thoughtfulness
Tranquility
Trust
Trustworthy
Understanding
Unique
Unselfish
Useful
Variety
Vitality
Warmhearted
Wealth
Wholehearted
Wisdom
Wonder
Zeal

Unit III

Making Love Work

- Living Where the Love Is

- Love: The Ultimate Power

- To Know Me Is to Love Me

8

Living Where the Love Is

Throughout the centuries love has been the inspiration for and the topic of hundreds of thousands of books, plays, poems, and songs. Love stimulates us, motivates us, challenges us, and often eludes us. Both the New and the Old Testaments command us to love our neighbors, and Jesus even went so far as to tell us to love our enemies.

Yet every neighborhood has its feuds, and some of us have trouble loving our *families*, let alone our enemies. There will always be people who "rub us the wrong way," and often we find those who most *need* love are the most unlovable. Is it possible to love everybody?

If we get hung up on the idea of whether we can love *everybody,* we will miss the fact that we *can* love *anybody* we choose to love. Love is a choice—not a feeling. Indeed, genuine love sometimes goes *against* our feelings.

It's easy, for example, to have compassion for nice people who are suffering difficulties. Anybody can love nice people. But to love people who do "un-nice" things, to have compassion for people whom we consider unlovable—that's true compassion. That's genuine love, and it's tough.

Some time ago, I remember saying to my wife, Simone, "I really want to love you unconditionally, and quite frankly, I am finding it difficult!" When you read that statement, did you wonder what kind of person *she* must be, to make it difficult, or what kind of person *I* must be, to find it difficult?

Well, I *certainly* hope your attention went to her, because she's *obviously* the problem. She has *all* these habits that irritate me! And I've talked to her about every one of them! I have *promised* her that as soon as she cleans up her act, I will love her *unconditionally.* And I'm a man of my word! (I hope you haven't missed my sarcasm.)

Sometimes we want to love someone unconditionally and we find it difficult. But our difficulty has little to do with the other person. It has a lot to do with us. We are either loving, or we are unloving.

If I am a loving individual, if my circle is filled with love, love will flow out—you will receive my love. If I am a hateful individual and you enter my life, you are going to experience some of my hate. I cannot love John and hate Bud and love Carol and hate Jane, because I'm either loving or I'm not. But, there are degrees of love, and none of us loves everybody to the same degree.

Living Above the Line

Let's suppose, for example, that in our lives there is a neutral, horizontal line. Everything above the line generally stems from love. It is positive, creative, harmonious. It is unity and light. Everything below the line stems primarily from fear. It is negative, destructive, dissonant. It is darkness and division. (See Figure 4.)

Each time we meet new people or new situations, we meet them on the line. During the first encounter, we will either place them above the line or below it. The higher above the line we place people, the more intense the degree of love we have for them. The farther below the line we place them, the stronger our fear and the more destructive our attitudes will be toward them.

+	love	light	creativity	unity	harmony
−	fear	darkness	destructiveness	division	dissonance

Figure 4.

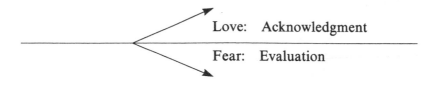

Love: Acknowledgment

Fear: Evaluation

Figure 5.

When we encounter a situation or individual new to us, we will respond automatically with at least an acknowledgment, which puts them above the line (positive) or an evaluation, which puts them below the line (negative). (See Figure 5.) The importance of this first step is that we will *continue* in the direction we have started. Love and fear are a continuum; there are degrees.

Let's say, for example, that tonight you decide to eat dinner in a restaurant. When you arrive, you notice that there is a man sitting alone at a small corner table. He is eating a steak and lobster dinner. What does this tell you about the man?

The answers vary among people, but they generally respond by saying, "The man is lonely." "He is hungry." "He likes steak and lobster." "He's on an expense account." One woman even suggested, "He's available."

All of these statements are evaluations. We do not know whether the man is lonely. Perhaps he just finished taking twenty-six Cub Scouts to the zoo and decided to dine alone because he was ready for some peace and quiet. We cannot even be sure he's hungry. Maybe he just finished a full-course dinner and somebody bet him fifty dollars he couldn't eat another one.

When we say he must be hungry or lonely or on an expense account, we are making an evaluation or a judgment, and our attitude is below the line. (We also discussed judgments in chapter 4.) The evaluation says *if I were doing* what he is doing, *I would be* lonely or hungry. If we acknowledge the situation, we simply say, "The man is eating a steak and lobster dinner." And our attitude is above the line.

Let's look at another example. What if I come home at the end of a day and my wife greets me with some information like this:

"Mary Jane called today and spent two hours telling me her troubles. Kevin fell off the stool again and smashed his nose. And I wasn't able to finish that typing I promised, because the man never did come to fix the machine."

Now, I can take that information above or below the line. If my attitude goes below the line with an evaluation, it might sound like this: "Why didn't you hang up on her? Tell her you're busy. If you had kept that stool where it belongs, he wouldn't have been up on it in the first place!" (Incidentally, I'm priding myself on my honesty!) What I don't understand is why she gets so upset with me when I'm just telling it like it is! Evaluations, advice, and unsolicited opinions have a unique way of shutting off communication.

I can take that same information above the line, and it could sound like this: "It sounds like you had a real busy day. I know what that's like." Acknowledgment and empathy have a unique way of keeping communication open.

At first glance, evaluation seems and sounds innocent. Are we making too big a deal out of it? We must consider initial evaluation serious because of *where it takes us*. In the following chart, notice how each step below the line is increasingly destructive.

+   acknowledgment

−   evaluation of event
       evaluation of person
       rationalization (criticism)
       doubt
       suspicion
       greed
       jealousy
       hate
       fear
       indifference

Figure 6.

Let me take you below the line step by step, with an illustration. A salesman goes out to make a presentation, and for whatever reason, he loses the sale. An *acknowledgment* is, "I lost the sale." But in this case, the man is fearful because of the loss and wants to have control over the situation.

He decides to:

EVALUATE THE EVENT: "I think I'd better go back to the office and try to figure out what went wrong."

EVALUATE THE BEING: "Maybe I wasn't friendly enough."

RATIONALIZE (Seek to justify): "Of course, I'm not always the friendly type."

DOUBT: "I sometimes wonder why I ever got started in this business in the first place."

SUSPICION: "I think the other salesmen are getting all the good leads anyway."

GREED: "That's why I'm going broke."

JEALOUSY: "They get all the applause, the accolades, the attention, the awards."

HATE: "That's why I can't stand them."

FEAR: "With people like that around, you can't make it in this business."

INDIFFERENCE: "Might as well quit. Who cares, anyway?"

You probably won't deteriorate that rapidly because of a single lost sale, but being judgmental does take us below the line, and the continuum begins. Because we tend to see others as we see ourselves, we usually put them on the same spot above or below the line as we find ourselves. Over a period of time, the downward trend of evaluation has eroded and destroyed our relationships and we've never known why.

In order to give us more understanding as to how this process works, I want to give you another illustration on a personal event. Here's the event: a man's wife comes home with a brand-new hairstyle.

EVALUATE THE EVENT: "My, you look nice. I like your hair better than before." (He thinks it's a compliment.)

EVALUATE THE PERSON: "It makes your face look nicer." (He still thinks he's paying her a compliment.)

RATIONALIZE (Seek to justify): "Your nose doesn't seem quite so large."

DOUBT: "You really can't disguise your nose, though."

SUSPICION: "Sometimes I think you tricked me into marrying you with a nose like that."

GREED: "Now, I have to spend my whole life with you and that nose."

JEALOUSY: "I sure know a lot of guys whose wives don't have large noses."

HATE: "I can hardly stand to be around you anymore."

FEAR: "You probably don't like me anyway."

INDIFFERENCE: "We really don't have anything going for us anyhow. I might as well leave."

If you find it difficult to break the evaluation habit which puts your feelings and attitudes into the fear syndrome, maybe this will help. First, remember that every thought below the line is negative. Negative thoughts create negative body chemistry, and negative body chemistry leads to death. For every minute you spend below the line in fear, it takes approximately twelve minutes above the line with a positive attitude *just to neutralize it.* Everything below the line is in your *imagination,* but it's so *real* it can kill you.

In his book *In Tune With the Infinite,* Ralph Waldo Trine tells a story about a mother who had been dominated for a few moments by an intense passion of anger. She was nursing a child at the time and within an hour of her angry experience the child at her breast died, so poisoned became the mother's milk by virtue of the poisonous secretions of the system while under the domination of this fit of anger. In other cases it has caused severe illness and convulsions.

To be great lovers we must make a commitment to live above

the line, in the positive, healing element of love. The first step is to simply begin to acknowledge what is. To recognize everybody's right to BE.

Have you ever tried to pretend someone didn't exist? You ignored them? You walked along the sidewalk pretending you didn't see them? I'm reminded of the little girl whose pigtails were pulled all morning in class. When she had taken all she could handle, she turned to the boy behind her and said, "If you existed, I'd speak to you."

If it seems strange to pretend that somebody doesn't exist or have the *right* to exist, consider the fact that on a national level, the United States government refused to recognize the People's Republic of China for nearly a quarter of a century. Now that we have acknowledged them, we've spent more than a decade building a relationship with them. Politics is not the issue here; what is important is that if we want to have relationships with others, we must begin with acknowledgment.

Once I begin to acknowledge another human being, the direction of the relationship tends to climb higher above the line. Those whom I acknowledge, I can accept. Whomever I can accept, I can approve, then appreciate, then admire, then adore—and finally—love unconditionally.

To understand the degrees of love above the line, let's look at the continuum as a triangle.

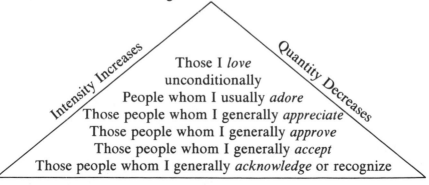

Figure 7.

We probably acknowledge many of the people we encounter in our daily lives, but we accept fewer of them. We appreciate a smaller number of people than we accept, and with each step up we find fewer people. At the top, we find that we love only a handful of people—or perhaps only one or two—unconditionally, but the intensity of our love is at its highest level.

All of us have placed some of the people in our lives above the line and some below the line. What is the difference? Why do we place some above the line and some below? It all goes back to *being* and *doing*. People in our lives who are below the line are there because of what *they do*. Those above the line are there because of who *they are,* in spite of what they do.

I ACKNOWLEDGE WHAT IS
WITHOUT MAKING VALUE JUDGMENTS

For example, the ability to distinguish between being and doing can enable a young man to love his father in spite of the fact that his dad drinks too much. If the young man couldn't make the distinction, he would probably label his father a drunken bum and break the relationship. But if the son does distinguish between who his father is and what his father does, he can acknowledge and accept his dad as a human being with a problem. Relationship is the key.

If your children do something "ornery," they're just kids. If the neighbor's children do the same thing, they're "brats." Most of us are familiar with the saying, "He's not heavy; he's my brother." Now we all know that heavy is heavy, but in a special relationship he doesn't seem heavy.

Have you ever had an experience like this? You're sitting in your car at an intersection, when you get a pretty hefty jolt from the rear. Somebody's really banged your bumper. Your immediate reaction is to swing around and yell out, "Why don't you. . . ."

And only then do you notice that the person who banged your car is a friend. Everything begins to change. "Oh, hi. I didn't recognize you at first. That really scared me. How have you been? I suppose we should get out and check for any damage." The whole incident settles down to nothing. Why do we behave differently with different people?

The key is *relationship* and that revolves around the kind of person *I am* and how I *value the other person.* If you have a relationship with a person, his behavior is virtually irrelevant. If you don't have a relationship, his behavior is the main issue.

Another way to live above the line is to see ourselves and others as highly valuable, as unrepeatable miracles. None of us is an accident. We would all be difficult to replace. We were created with design, and our lives have unique purposes. Life is expecting something special from me that only I can give.

I AM AN UNREPEATABLE MIRACLE

We treat people and things according to how we value them. Recently a man was driving down the freeway, pulling a horse trailer. In the trailer was a horse worth about $25,000, and the man was tense and nervous. He gripped the steering wheel with clenched fists, and perspiration ran down his face. His friend turned to him and said, "Man, why are you so nervous?"

"I've never had anything this valuable in my car before." With a look of incredulity, his friend replied, "I've been in your car many times before, and you never drove this carefully!"

How would it make *you* feel if someone didn't think you were as valuable as a horse? But how often are we guilty of the same sort of thing? Did you ever notice that a man will race down the freeway with his family, tailgating, cutting in and out of traffic, and taking all kinds of chances? But if he's towing a trailer or a boat or a camper, he really tries to be careful?

If it's true that we treat everything according to how we value it, let me give you a little test to check on how you value yourself. Let's pretend that I'm going to give you a dog to take care of for the next thirty days. Now he's not just any dog. He's purebred, registered, and has won many blue ribbons. He cost me a thousand dollars. He's very valuable. How do you suppose you would take care of such an animal?

Would you feed him regularly? Or would you rush him through his meals with an occasional "better yet, bring it with you." Would you see that he was fed a well-balanced diet? Or would you let him eat anything he liked—especially if he whined a little. Would you let him get overweight? Would you keep him up all night at wild parties, making him neurotic? Would you wake him up every morning with a cigarette and a cup of black coffee? "Come on, Fido, up and at 'em. Get your adrenaline going!"

I have to believe that most people reading this are thinking, *Nobody who really loved a dog would ever treat him that way.* And he's just a dog.

To get in touch with how you value yourself, think about how you have treated yourself for the past thirty days.

If we're living above the line, the value we place upon ourselves and others will be above the line, too. As valuable human beings, we will treat ourselves and others with compassion.

When we're living above the line, we will take the people and the situations we encounter as high on the chart as we possibly can. The very least we can do with anybody is acknowledge them. That's a long way from adoration, but it's above the line. It's a place to start. I think that most of us would admit that we can acknowledge *anybody*—if we choose to. In perspective, that means that if we can acknowledge anybody, *we can love anybody.* We have a choice. Love is a decision.

If we acknowledge someone long enough, we might be able to move up to acceptance. If we accept them for a while, we might begin to approve. And, behold, someday we might find ourselves actually appreciating someone. Appreciating them today, when we could barely acknowledge them yesterday.

Where will you put your spouse? Above or below the line? That's probably fairly easy. (I hope it's above the line!) If you have an ex-spouse it may be more difficult. If, in your mind, your ex-spouse is below the line, where is that going to put you? What about your children? They each deserve to be kept above the line no matter what they do. Where would you put your boss? How about the people who work with you or for you? Or your neighbors?

This story is told of Eddie Rickenbacker, who was the leading American air ace during World War I. During World War II, he went on an inspection tour on behalf of the secretary of war. About six hundred miles north of Samoa, his airplane was forced down into the Pacific Ocean. With seven other survivors, Rickenbacker floated aimlessly in a rubber life raft for twenty-four days.

As the days drifted into weeks, the men slipped farther and farther below the line. Finally they edged into psychological withdrawal, which spelled doom for them all. Rickenbacker knew there was only one way to keep the men alive. His was a lonely decision, but it took a man who lived above the line to do it.

He needled them. Provoked them. Slapped them. Eventually he enraged them so much that he was able to bring them up from indifference to hatred. The hatred created adrenalin and saved their lives.

Normally we do not think that making somebody hate is the most loving thing we can do. But, again, the most loving thing most of us will ever do in our lives will probably be the hardest, because it will go against our feelings.

Let me pull some ideas into focus. In chapter 4, we said that everything we do is to *get* love or *because* we're loved. In other words, we do what we do to get what is *above the line,* that is, acknowledgment, acceptance, approval, or we do what we do because we have what is above the line.

In that same chapter we talked about how to break the performance-for-love syndrome by giving people what they need (what's above the line) unrelated to what they are doing. This will give you a better idea as to how to make that happen.

And, then in chapter 2, the question was asked, "How do we get rid of fear?" (Now identified as what is below the line.) And the answer was, "Focus and concentrate on love." (Now identified as what is above the line.)

If you will allow your mind to only focus and dwell on the love that is above the line, the fear that is below the line will begin to vanish. "Perfect love casts out fear." You can live without fear! You can be one who loves.

Step Eight to Becoming a Great Lover: I put everything and everybody in my life above the line.

Workshop:

1. Check your Self-Esteem Exercise for how you answered questions 24, 35, 36, 43, and 46.
2. What docs it mean to live above the line?
3. What is the first step in learning how to love?
4. Why do we put some people above the line and others below?
5. What do we do for people when we put them above the line?
6. What happens to me when I spend any time below the line?
7. In our vocations, we sometimes strive and fail. Then we have a tendency to analyze what went wrong, dwell on it, and begin to doubt ourselves. What should we do instead?
8. Listed are several events. Give them an acknowledgment and an evaluation.

   Event: In a tennis game, you hit the ball out-of-bounds.

   Acknowledge: _____

   Evaluate: _____

   Event: Someone tells you a lie.

   Acknowledge: _____

   Evaluate: _____

   Event: You experience disappointment in a venture.

   Acknowledge: _____

   Evaluate: _____

9

Love: The Ultimate Power

Some time ago I happened to catch a "Happy Days" television episode when Mork of "The Mork and Mindy Show" was visiting the Cunningham household. If you have ever watched "Mork and Mindy," you know that Mork is an alien from another planet with an extraordinary ability to do strange things, even with his fingers.

In this particular episode, Mork agreed to give Richie Cunningham and his friends some of his unusual ability. Touching their fingertips, he transferred some of his power to them. Immediately they began using it to make people do strange things, such as dance on tables, turn cartwheels, and act foolishly in general. After about thirty seconds of this, Mork cried out, "Stop! You are abusing the power! Give it back!"

Several days later I read an interesting advertisement regarding the film *Caligula*. The story details the life of the debauched young Roman emperor, Nero. The advertisement asked, "What would you have done if you had been given absolute power of life and death over everybody else in the whole world?"

I pondered that question for some time. It seems to me that many of us have the idea that the chance to play God would be a great opportunity because it not only represents love, it also represents power. If how we handle power is the major factor in revealing whether we are good or evil, the real test may be less in how we use power and more in how we *don't* use it.

We seem to want power—to be in control, to pull all the strings. In our relationships, on the job, in our homes, with our friends, we find ourselves in kind of an emotional and psychological tug-of-war.

We all want power, but we're also afraid of people who have it, because they then have the opportunity to take advantage of us or manipulate us. This is why our own neediness scares us. To be needy is to be in the weak position. Who can you trust with power?

Let's work on that question by looking at the relationship between two definitions. The first is *Success:* The ability to establish long-lasting relationships with people. The second is *Love:* The commitment of my will to meet your needs and best interests, regardless of how I feel.

Can I establish a long-lasting relationship without committing my will to meet your needs and best interests? I think not. (Incidentally, in business, "long-lasting relationship" translates into repeats and referrals.) If you and I wanted to build a relationship based on this definition, how would you know that I really cared for you? If I were willing to put your needs and best interests ahead of mine, you would know. And I want you to know that I am willing to do just that. I *really* am . . . just as soon as you do!

Don't Be Afraid to Go First

Does that sound familiar? I think it gives us a great clue to one of the major problems in relationships. We all know what love requires, but we are *afraid to go first.* And so the power struggle begins. We have all experienced initiating trust in a relationship and, consequently, being taken advantage of. Some have been so disillusioned, they have vowed never to risk it again.

When no one is willing to take the first step, we look for a compromise. "Let's both go first. I'll meet you halfway. But don't go too fast. I want to keep this relationship even—fifty-fifty." Is a fifty-fifty relationship what love is all about?

Isn't love a commitment forever, a permanent thing, a life-wager—not as-long-as, or until anything. Doesn't love mean the unreserved giving of myself for the benefit of the other, even if it costs me my life? Now we're beginning to understand why love is so scary. To love "all the way" is to put your ego, your reputation, your very life on the line.

"What if I make that kind of commitment and fail? I'll look like a fool. It's too risky. How about a seventy-thirty deal? That way I can hedge my bet. I've got to protect my ego in case it doesn't work out."

So, with the fear of commitment in a relationship, we have developed a very convenient arrangement called a "trial marriage." A trial marriage simply means we don't want to make any long-range commitments. We want to hang loose with all our options open. We want to keep one foot in the door—just in case.

After about six months or so, what do you almost inevitably hear? "Well, it didn't work out. I was afraid it wouldn't. I'm sure glad I kept my foot in the door."

At this point I'm going to assume that most people are smart enough to know that you can't go all the way in a relationship with your foot in the door. This applies, of course, to both our personal and professional lives.

With words like *commitment* and *needs* and *interests* and *power* and *long-term relationships* in mind, let's look at some of the relationships in which we might be involved, considering the question, "Who goes first to meet the other's need?" In every relationship—sales–client, manager–subordinate, husband–wife—there is a need on the part of each that must be met in order for the relationship to be successful.

Whenever I freely give the other what he needs, I am acting lovingly and strengthening the relationship. Whenever I deliberately withhold in a power play what the other needs, I have acted malevolently, overwhelmed by the fear of my own needs, and have weakened the relationship.

A manager, for example, can give the pay increase that is deserved (meeting the need) or can make the subordinate grovel. A salesperson can take advantage of a customer's need when demand is greater than supply by raising the price of his product. In the bedroom, one partner can refrain from meeting the sexual needs of the other as a way of controlling the relationship.

Recently I had occasion to purchase a new automobile. Because of the economy, the supply was greater than the demand, and it was a buyer's market. I knew the dealer was hurting and needy and that I was in the position of power. I was faced with a decision.

I could remember the times when I have been in the position of need and others took advantage of me. I could use this opportunity as a way of working out my resentment—to even the score a little bit. My alternative as one who wants to be a great lover was simply to seek an agreement that would be fair to both of us.

Love never takes advantage of a person in a needy position, but it has very little to do with the situation or the other person. It has everything to do with the kind of person I am.

Disraeli said, "Next to knowing when to seize an opportunity, the most important thing in life is to know when to forego an advantage."

I CAN BE TRUSTED
TO USE MY POWER
FOR THE GOOD OF OTHERS

Who Can You Trust?

Several years ago we were living in a house that had become too small for our growing family. Because we needed more room, we considered the options of adding on to our present property or buying a bigger house instead. Our initial decision was to buy the bigger house, so we made arrangements to meet with a broker in our neighborhood.

The following Saturday morning our broker sat with us in our living room for about an hour. He asked questions and made notations on his yellow legal pad. The purpose of his time with us was to determine what our needs were and how they could best be met.

At the end of the hour, he said, "I would really like to have your listing, Mr. Grant, but I think you should stay here and add on to your property. It will be better for you." We took the broker's advice and stayed where we were. We added on several rooms, and it *has* turned out to be the best investment for our money. (Remember the building project in chapter 2?)

A "hungry" salesman who was primarily interested in his own needs would not have encouraged us to stay put. Most salesmen would have walked right in and made every effort to secure the listing of the property before assessing the need.

Although our broker didn't make any money for himself that day, he has earned several commissions since then from the people we have sent to him because he is a salesman who can be trusted. His willingness to give us what we needed in spite of his own financial concerns paid off for all of us in the long run.

LOVE THINKS LONG-RANGE

Recently I had the need to meet with an estate planner, which is just a fancy name for an insurance salesman. During our appointment, he described several plans for me. Of those various plans, which do you think he wanted to sell me? When I've asked that question in a seminar setting, the overwhelming response has been, "The most expensive!" Who do you suppose taught people to think that way? Probably the kinds of salesmen who practice the adage, Let the buyer beware. But on this particular occasion, I believe the salesman had my best interest at heart. He seemed to believe in the motto, Let the buyer be served. We drew up a plan that best met the needs of my family.

About twelve years ago I had an estate planner who sold me a program that was really in *his* best interest. From the program he sold me, he received a very large commission up front, right off the top. The plan turned out to be something that I could not handle, and at the end of a year, I had to drop it. If that salesman had been more interested in my needs than his, he would probably have had my business for the last twelve years rather than for just the one year. And, of course, in the long run, twelve years of business would have been better than just the one. He sacrificed the permanent on the altar of the immediate.

IMMATURITY IS ACUTE
SHORTSIGHTEDNESS

It is very difficult to think of the needs of others when we are overwhelmed with our own—and most of us *are* preoccupied with our own needs. It is quite natural then that we should seek out relationships in which we can have our needs met, rather than those in which we can contribute to the relationship.

In a sales–customer relationship, our principle would say that the salesperson was committed to go first in meeting the needs of the customer. If a customer believes that the salesperson is out primarily to meet his own needs (and most customers believe that), then it is next to impossible to establish a relationship of trust. Without trust there can be no repeat or referral business.

At a recent sales meeting I encouraged the people to leave the meeting thinking and believing, *Everybody I meet today needs me. They love me. They trust me. And because they trust me they will believe what I tell them.*

A guy in the back of the room yelled, "That's when you zap 'em!"

Have you ever been "zapped," or taken advantage of? Twice? Not likely.

However, we do have to admit that you can make a lot of money in business zapping people. But in case you haven't discovered it, you're working too hard. You have to keep finding new people to zap!

Some time ago, Chevrolet had an advertising campaign that I really liked. It said, "We don't want you for a season; we don't want you for a year; we want you for *keeps!*" Do you get clients for keeps by zapping them or by meeting their needs?

On most referral sales the trust factor is fairly high, probably because somebody's needs were met. I doubt if any salesperson has ever had a customer come to him and say, "I understand that you just took advantage of my neighbor and I would love to receive the same treatment!"

I want to share with you an interesting story regarding seasickness and neediness that may give you an insight as to why it is difficult to trust a "hungry" salesperson.

Every year the California grey whales migrate from the warm waters of the Baja Peninsula to the cold waters of the Bering Strait. During the migration the whales come within a mile or so of the California coastline. Because of this, a southern California pastime known as "whale watching" has developed. When migration begins, people can arrange for a boat to take them about a mile out to sea where they can watch the whales. The boats are able to maneuver within a few yards of these thirty-ton sea mammals.

The day my family went out, the water was rough and choppy. A number of people became seasick. Seasickness is a dreadful experience because there is no escape, nowhere to go for help. Some of the people were suffering such agony that they were curled up in the fetal position, immobile. (They tell me that with seasickness you have two fears: the first is that you are going to die; the second is that you're *not* going to die.)

What do you suppose the response would be if I approached one of these very sick people and said, "I don't mean to bother you, but I've really got a bad headache."

I imagine their response would have been something like, "Go away, don't bother me. Leave me alone." Another possible response might be simply, "Drop dead!"

And what if I replied to that with, "You're so darn selfish. You're all wrapped up in yourself. You're an egomaniac. You obviously don't care about anyone else."

I think it is obvious that it is very difficult to think about someone else's needs when you are overwhelmed with your own. But, don't go away. I want to tell you about an interesting psychological phenomenon that can solve the problem.

What if one of those seasick persons was a mother or father who had a child suddenly swept overboard into the sea? What would happen to the seasickness? In most cases it would immediately disappear. Why? Because their attention and focus was on a *greater* need. Here's the principle: If you focus your attention on a greater need, you will get better. If you focus your attention on your own needs, you will get sicker. When you throw your energies into outside activities and devote yourself to other people and their interests, you normally will tend to feel less concerned with your own needs. The giving of love has a marvelous way of healing both the giver and the receiver.

A genuine interest in others is a difficult quality to develop. If a person has been shaped for the first twenty-five years of their career by self-interest incentives—not to mention their educational career with grades and awards and accolades—it will be a struggle for them to have an adequate vision of the needs and dreams of others. Yet because all relationships are potential power struggles, the truly great lover is willing to risk going first—again and again.

Meeting the needs of others as a key to successful relationships is certainly not a new idea.

I recently had an occasion to speak in San Francisco. As I entered the building where the meeting was to be held, I noticed a marble plaque by the front door with this inscription:

A. P. Giannini   1870–1949
A. P. Giannini founded Bank of Italy in San Francisco in 1904 to "Serve the needs of others—the only legitimate business in the world today." His devotion to this far-sighted philosophy revolu-

tionized the face of banking, and he lived to see his "bank for the little fellows" become Bank of America, the largest bank in the world today. To his philosophy of service for all, this building and all who work for the Bank he inspired are dedicated.

What made Giannini's efforts so successful? I believe it was a combination of commitment, responsibility, and genuine interest in the needs of others. All three qualities fall under a conscientious willingness to take the first step in meeting the needs of others.

Simone and I have four children, three girls and a boy. The boy, Kevin, is the youngest. A few years ago when Simone and I would go out for an evening, Kevin would beg to be the baby-sitter.

"Why do you want to be the baby-sitter, Kevin?" Simone asked one night.

"Because I want to be the boss!"

"What does the boss do?" I queried.

"The boss tells people what to do. I get to stay up late and watch TV, and everybody else has to go to bed. When they're the boss, I have to get everything they want. Now I'm going to make them get things for me!"

When I tried to explain to Kevin what it really meant to be a baby-sitter—to be responsible and accountable, to meet other people's needs, to serve, to be the last one to go down with the ship if necessary—he wasn't interested. He wanted the power and the authority, but he was unwilling to hear anything about responsibility.

There needs to be a balance between power and responsibility, and love supplies that balance. The two really are a unit, because without responsibility, authority becomes a dictator. Whenever a great lover is in the authority position in a relationship, he uses that position to serve.

A successful manager, for example, strives to develop successful employees. He gives himself away for the sake of his people, because he realizes he is not truly successful unless he wants his people to know more and do better than himself. When he has a genuine interest in other people and their needs, they owe him nothing.

THERE IS NO LIMIT TO WHAT A PERSON CAN DO IF HE DOESN'T CARE WHO GETS THE CREDIT

Between a parent and child, it is expected that the parent will go first to meet the needs of the child. This, of course, is one of the most basic sacrifices of mankind. Yet the goal of these sacrifices is to bring the child from zero responsibility to 100 percent responsibility—to full maturity. It is interesting that when the child reaches maturity and responsible adulthood, nature often reverses the roles and it becomes the child's responsibility to go first to meet the needs of the parent.

One of the risky aspects of being in authority is the necessity of delegating responsibility to others. Some people seem to be willing to give responsibility, but they stop short of providing the authority to go with it.

An example of this is the teacher–student relationship. One of the major problems in our educational system today is that teachers have been given an enormous responsibility with very little authority. A lot of students are demanding authority with very little responsibility. It won't work. We need to return to the teachers the authority that is commensurate with their responsibility.

But the problem doesn't stop with the educational system. Recently I was talking with the president of a company, and he shared with me the common complaint of middle management: responsibility without authority. One of his managers had expressed his frustration by saying, "You give me a gun, but you don't give me any bullets."

"If I had given you any bullets," the president replied, "you would probably have killed everybody." My comment to the president was, "If you can't trust your people with the reality of authority, don't frustrate them with the symbolism of responsibility."

On the other hand, I frequently have had salesmen ask me, "Why doesn't management give us any say? We're out on the battlefield with the troops. We know what's going on; why don't they let us call the shots?"

So I ask the salesmen, "If you are given the authority to call your own shots and make your own decisions, are you willing to accept the full responsibility for those decisions?" At that point, the immature will back down, but those with maturity won't. People in authority can "go first" by allowing their subordinates to make those kinds of decisions. They must be allowed to make some mistakes. Responsibility is the path to maturity.

Authority and responsibility also have a lot to do with the relationship of parents and children, especially teenagers. As children start moving through adolescence, they want more and more authority, but they're not too eager for responsibility. They want to make their own decisions. They don't want Dad and Mom telling them what to do.

Until the child reaches legal age, I think the parent needs to take this approach: "As long as you are under our roof and we have any responsibility for you, we also have the authority that goes with it. If you don't like that arrangement, then you can go out into the world and build your own roof and under that roof you can be your own authority and make all of your own decisions. But you must understand, that along with the authority you will also have *full* responsibility—including the *finances.*" That usually slows them down. Don't fall into the trap of allowing them to move under their own roof, be their own authority, but still try to hold you responsible.

Do people who are *not* in the authority position have any power? Yes, the power of submission. It's difficult for us to accept the idea of submission because we think of it as weakness or inferiority. That is truly unfortunate, because in the context of unconditional love, submission is a good deal of power. What may appear subservient from one point of view is the main purpose from another.

It takes strength—not weakness—to surrender a part of my sovereignty. It takes courage, not cowardice, to give my life unreservedly for the benefit of another human being. It takes an eloquent selflessness to have genuine interest in others—especially when my own needs may be so great.

Love Is Not Afraid to Lose

In all relationships, someone has to initiate the bond of trust. The question of "who goes first" is settled with one principle: **Love will not debate it.**

The principle of love is a principle of power. Not the self-seeking power that plays on the neediness of others. Not the self-protective power that prefers compromise to commitment. Not the demanding, authoritative kind of power—but the trustworthy power that reaches out to serve the needs of others.

Great lovers are not involved in a power struggle. They are in loving relationships of interdependence. The consideration of equality or who goes first does not arise. It's not a worrisome struggle, but a giving and receiving, symbolized by what C. S. Lewis described as "an infectiously festive occasion, with the image of dancing." Some dancers must bow to their partners, some must lead, and some must follow. What is especially interesting about the image is that those who lead now may have to follow as the dance moves on. To participate in the dance is to abdicate (power) continually and continually to be raised. The dance is a picture of unison of individuals in which freedom and order are harmoniously combined. The freedom and spontaneity of the dance do not stand in tension with the order and precision it requires. The image of dancing sees each participant entering into the festive spirit of the dance only when he freely submits to its rules. It is what Lewis called the reconciliation of boundless freedom with order.

A story that might help us to understand power and trust and leadership that serves is Rudolph the Red-Nosed Reindeer. A couple of years ago, I saw the Japanese television production of this famous story. What made Rudolph unique was that he was given this special *power* that caused his nose to light up, and because of this special power he was able to be a *leader*. In this particular version he was given this special power with the admonition that he was to use it only for *good.* Rudolph was warned that if he ever used his power for an evil purpose, he would lose it immediately.

In the story Rudolph is tricked (deceived?) into using his power to light up an office so some people can steal some money. The next time he attempts to use his power, he discovers it's gone!

Let's pretend. I'm going to give you all the power you need to be what you want to be and to do what you want to do. There are no limits as long as you use your power for good—in the best interests of other people. But if just once you use your power for anything selfish, unloving, or evil, you will immediately lose it. How long do you think you will keep the power? Can you be trusted?

Remember the advertisement? "What would you have done if you had been given absolute power of life and death over everybody else in the whole world?" Why don't you just pause a moment and ponder that question.

Only Absolute Good can have Absolute Power.

If you had the power to break up a few fish and a few loaves of bread to feed the hungry multitudes, could you be trusted not to exploit it?

If you had the power to turn water into wine, could you be trusted not to go into a commercial venture?

If you had the power to throw yourself off a high place and not be harmed, would you be tempted to try and prove it?

If you were offered all the kingdoms of the world, would you sell out? They say that every person has his price!

How we *don't* use power may be the greatest revelation of who we really are. Power that is used for self-preservation cannot be trusted. Power that is used to serve the needs of others can be trusted. Only then will the power struggle cease. Release what you think is the key to your power so you can find out where the real dynamic of love is.

Step Nine to Becoming a Great Lover: I can be trusted to use my power to serve the needs of others.

Workshop:

1. Check with your Values Inventory to see how you answered questions 12 and 13. Do you have any personal power? And how have you used it in the last forty-eight hours? Benevolently or malevolently?
2. Why are most relationships a power struggle?
3. What does it take for the power struggle to cease?
4. What does our handling of power reveal about us?
5. How does love supply the balance between authority and responsibility?
6. In terms of authority and responsibility, think about the number one fear of top management (delegation) and the number one problem of middle management (responsibility without authority).
7. What does it mean to say that "Immaturity is acute short-sightedness"?
8. Think of the many roles you have during a week: boss, subordinate, student, teacher, salesperson, client, waiter, customer, driver, passenger, husband, wife, parent, child, and so on. When you are in an authority role, do you serve lovingly, and when you are in a role to be served do you receive graciously? Do you know how to dance?

10

To Know Me Is to Love Me

All human beings have universal needs in addition to the physical essentials of food and shelter. We all require a sense of well-being and a certain amount of affection, for example. We need to be respected and to have skills. We need power to make our own choices and a sense of responsibility to balance the power. We must be free to learn, and we require economic and psychological stability.

When we are deprived of these basic necessities, we become anxious, frustrated, unhealthy people who are motivated mainly by fear. When those needs are fulfilled, we are developing to our fullest potential. We can then become mature, integrated individuals who are motivated by love.

All of us have certain life-styles and behavior patterns which stem from our needs. The personality patterns we develop can be grouped loosely into several categories, each of which has characteristic needs and fears additional to those we've already mentioned. When we recognize and understand those needs and fears, we can build better relationships with people in each category.

Five Personality Groups

There are five general personality groups, and each has its own way of dealing with life. We can face life apathetically, aggressively, analytically, adaptively, or we can deal with life as an integrated person, a "self-actualizer." In a way, these are all stages of growth, because they closely resemble the normal physical and chronological progression of childhood.

When a baby is born, he is basically *apathetic*. He cannot be concerned about the events occurring in the world because he is unaware of them. He cries when he is uncomfortable or in need of affection, but he is totally indifferent to the needs and desires of his parents and siblings. He is the center of his own world.

From toddlerhood through middle childhood, we see an *aggressive* pattern. The child is still the center of his own world, but he feels a need to defend it. The first word he seems to learn is *No!* and the second word is often *Mine!* which is his way of seeking control of his world.

It is in the early and middle childhood years that he learns to argue and debate, and in times of frustration he will resort to physical expressions of anger. He'll hit, bite, kick, scream, and slam doors. While a child of this age is aware of his own feelings, it is difficult for him to be concerned about the feelings of others.

As the child approaches junior high school, he becomes *analytical*. He sees everything in detail and insists on specifics. He requires, for instance, that his parents tell him exactly what they expect of him. He is not satisfied with a mere, "Clean your room." Instead, he requires step-by-step instruction: "Make your bed. Dust the furniture. Put your dirty clothes in the hamper, and vacuum the floor, please." The preteen and young teenager will remind his parents of every promise or near-promise, citing how it was spoken, when it was said, and where everyone was when they said it.

By the time a child reaches his later teen years, he has usually become *adaptive*. Peer pressure is at its strongest, and it is at this stage that the "system" has its most powerful effects. The most frequently used expression of the adaptive teenager seems to be "Everybody else is doing it." Conformity is the name of the game, and even in rebellion there is little diversity of expression.

One would hope, having progressed through these stages, that somewhere around the age of twenty-one we might be able to get it all together—to become fully integrated or "self-actualized." Somehow, it rarely happens. Abraham Maslow, who developed the idea of the self-actualized personality and the hierarchy of need structure, said that he knew of no self-actualized persons younger than sixty years of age, and even those were a very small number.[1]

Some of us complete the stages and revert to one of the earlier ways of handling life. Some of us reach one stage or another and settle in, never growing past it. Some of us operate from all of the stages at different times.

We Are All Personality Blends

It is important here to emphasize that none of us can be placed in a box and labeled as one of these types to the exclusion of the others. There are no exact lines; there are shades and overlaps. Yet there are strong general tendencies, too, and understanding these stages in terms of basic personality profiles can help us to understand ourselves and the people we encounter.

Whenever we deal with people, we begin to notice patterns of behavior and styles of conversation that seem to be predictable. Do you know anyone, for example, who will tell you the precise hour and minute when you ask him the time? Is there someone in your life who seems to talk through his teeth—who expresses himself in terms of power and strength and force? Do you have a friend who rarely remembers details and frequently answers your questions in approximates? "It's after four." "Uncle John is coming to visit us for a while. He'll be here in a couple of weeks or so."

It would probably be a simple task to place the first two of these examples in one of the five categories, but most of us would be a little puzzled with the third. To help you discover the profile to which an individual may belong, I've developed an informal test. It involves four simple questions you can use naturally and easily in most conversations:

- Isn't it a beautiful day?
- What kind of work do you do?
- How do you like your job?
- Would you tell me about your children (or parents)?

---

1. Frank Goble, *The Third Force,* Grossman Publishers, New York, 1970, p. 24.

The way a person responds to those questions will reveal a great deal about his personality, his attitudes, and his life-style.

1. Apathetic. Let's look first at the way an apathetic person views his world. In response to the question, "Isn't it a beautiful day?" the apathetic person will probably say something like, "A day is a day. If you've seen one, you've seen them all." He works at any job he can get, although many apathetics are habitually unemployed. His response to the two questions about work will be a shrug and a statement like, "A job is a job. I do my job to get money, that's all."

An apathetic person sees kids as kids, jobs as jobs, and days as days. He rarely expresses opinions because he really doesn't care. His *basic need is to be left alone,* so his *basic fear is involvement.* In many respects he is as far below the line as a person can be; indifference is the clue.

2. Aggressive. An aggressive person is far from indifferent. He has strong feelings and opinions, and he doesn't mind telling you what they are. To the question, "Isn't it a beautiful day?" aggressives will react with an immediate argument. "No. It's a crummy day." Subconsciously he's saying, "You're not going to tell me what kind of a day it is."

Aggressive people are physical people. They're truck drivers, construction workers, police officers, and politicians. They'll say, "I've got a tough job. I work like a horse." If you ask them about their children, they'll emphasize the qualities of strength and power.

"Man, I've got a tough kid. Nobody pushes him around, that's for sure. He's going to be a linebacker, that one. He's rugged." It's a physical world; that's where the strength is, that's where *life* is. Survival is the key to existence.

The aggressive's needs are primarily physical. They need food, water, shelter, clothing, physical sex. Their house is well built, they like cement floors, brick walls, and perhaps iron grates at the windows. Emotionally and psychologically, they *need power, strength, and control,* because *losing control is their most basic fear.* It is anguish for an aggressive to lose an argument.

3. Analyticals. Analyticals rarely argue; they simply state the facts. An analytical person will answer your question, "Isn't it a beautiful day?" by giving you a weather report: "It's seventy-two degrees and the barometer is dropping. The wind is out of the north by northwest, and those are cumulus clouds."

This person has no simple answers and is uncomfortable with approximations. If you say it is 3 miles to town, he'll tell you it's 2.9. He's not trying to put you down, he's trying to be helpful. For the analytical, everything has to be precise.

Analyticals will tell you that their children don't always obey, but they "do know right from wrong." "Jason has a 4.0 average," they may tell you, "and Jill has a 3.2. She's probably going to earn five A's and two B's this quarter."

Analyticals are lovers of detail. They are engineers, architects, bankers, escrow officers, and accountants. When you ask them how they like their jobs, they will tell you about fringe benefits, retirement plans, and insurance programs. They'll remind you of their years of training and preparation, and tell you that good jobs don't "just happen."

Analyticals *need perfection*. Everything must be either black or white, and if they don't have all the facts and all the details, they become agitated. They are uncomfortable with ambiguity and loose ends, and their *greatest fear is that missing some important detail will cause them to fail.*

4. Adaptives. Adaptives *fear rejection* more than failure, because their greatest *need is for recognition, acknowledgment, and acceptance.* They fear they will not be able to function if others do not approve of them. Adaptives have no need to win or to control, and they have little interest in details. They are often able to meet the needs of the other personality types because they tend to be people-pleasers.

To the question, "Isn't it a beautiful day?" an adaptive will reply, "Do you think so? Do you like warm weather?" If you answer yes, the adaptive will say, "Me too." If you answer no, the adaptive will say, "I like it cooler myself."

Adaptives are usually in the "people" business. They are salespeople, doctors, nurses, clergymen, social workers, and people in high management. They are concerned about their co-workers, their clients, and their families, and they generally want everyone to be happy. They become uncomfortable if somebody upsets the apple cart.

5. Self-actualizers. Finally, there are the self-actualizers. Ask them how they feel about the day, and they'll tell you it's perfect, but weather has nothing to do with it. They live from the inside out and above the line. They acknowledge the weather, but they don't evaluate it.

They think their kids and parents are terrific, but they don't tell you why. They know what they want in life, and they know what to be to get it. They don't have deficiency needs as the other types have.

Self-actualizers can be found in any business or profession. They enjoy their careers, and if you ask them how they like their jobs, they'll say, "It's my *life*." They don't think of their occupations as work—they simply do what they like and get paid for it at the same time.

Most of us fall into one of the first three categories—aggressive, analytical, or adaptive. To have satisfactory relationships with these various personality types, we must choose to meet the psychological and emotional needs their personalities require. We acknowledge and accept people where they are, and we offer them what they need as much as possible without feeding the negatives.

For example, we will acknowledge the aggressive's need for control. We will allow him to be forceful in his expressions without being threatened by his intensity. If he disagrees with our view of the weather, we can respond by saying, "You're probably right, but I'm sure you can handle it." (And he's thinking to himself, *You're darn right I can handle it, and you're pretty smart to recognize it!*)

What we have done at this moment is to eliminate his fear of losing control by letting him win. When he does accept the possibility that there might be more than one viewpoint on a subject, we can support and affirm him in that.

We can meet the needs of the analytical by recognizing his need for detail. We can supply facts and figures for him whenever possible, and we can approve of his efforts even when they are not "perfect."

Because the adaptive is in need of recognition, we can eliminate his fears of rejection by acknowledging and accepting him. We can respect his thirst for social orientation and offer him our friendship just because of who he is. When an adaptive decides to do what he thinks is best in spite of opposition, we can encourage him.

What we are discussing here is the principle of living above the line. Notice in Figure 8 that the self-actualized and adaptive personality traits are generally above the line—they are motivated by love. Personality traits that are more analytical, aggressive, and apathetic are often below the line. They are motivated primarily by fear.

This isn't bad news. We need people in these areas. A policeman has to have a degree of paranoia to survive. He has to be aware that danger lurks around every corner when he's at work, or he can lose his life and endanger the public. Problems develop if he takes his work home with him and continues to be suspicious of everyone. If he is aware of his need, he'll be able to leave his very necessary job-related need at work and operate from love at home.

Engineers need their fear of ambiguity to do their jobs well. Every person who rides in a Boeing 747 is dependent upon an analytical's insistence that the design of that airplane be aerodynamically sound. But what happens when the analytical returns home and the checkbook doesn't balance? If he has left his need at work, he can quietly correct the mistakes in the book without attacking the person who made them. Along this line I'm reminded of a recent speech entitled "Books Will Balance; People Won't," which I did for a C.P.A. Convention.

If we truly want to grow, we will work at eliminating

SELF-ACTUALIZING			UNCONDITIONAL LOVE
(Value/Need) People Lovers			ADORATION
			ADMIRATION
ADAPTIVE			APPRECIATION
(People) People Pleasers			APPROVAL
			ACCEPTANCE
	+Being Love Light		ACKNOWLEDGMENT
	−Doing Fear Dark		EVALUATION (Event)
ANALYTICAL			
(Detail) People Watchers			EVALUATION (of person)
			RATIONALIZATION
			DOUBT
AGGRESSIVE			SUSPICION
(Physical) People Users			GREED
			JEALOUSY
APATHETIC			HATE
(Fear) People Isolaters			FEAR
			INDIFFERENCE

Figure 8.

hindrances when we recognize them. Recycling is one process. (In the appendix there is a list of growth inhibitors that you can check for recognition and recycling.) But how will we be able to tell that we are growing?

If you are an aggressive type of personality, you will know if you are growing when you can feel okay about yourself even though you are losing an argument. You will recognize growth when you are more willing to *resolve* a conflict than to win it, and when you purchase a car that is suitable for transportation but which does not reflect your need for power. Consider some other indicators for *aggressive* personalities:

I know I am growing when:
- I realize that there are times when people in authority over me rightfully have authority over me.
- I can risk getting close to people without feeling I have to control them or that I have lost control of my life.
- I recognize that there is possibly more than one way to perform a given task.
- I consider the feelings and expectations of other people rather than ignoring them and dismissing them perfunctorily.

If you are an analytical type of personality, you will know you are growing when you realize your checkbook doesn't balance, and you can leave it until morning and sleep well anyway. You'll recognize growth when you can accept and live with some generalities and approximations, and when you can purchase a major appliance without checking *every* detail of engineering, construction, and contract. Consider these additional indicators of growth for *analyticals:*

I know I am growing when:
- I replace "who is right and who is wrong" with "what is the best solution to this situation."
- I hear the entire conversation without clicking off in my mind to formulate a response.

- I can act to accomplish a task without having all the information I desire.
- I can acknowledge the error in the family checkbook without making the error a capital offense and perhaps rejecting the offender.

If you are an adaptive type, you will recognize growth when you are able to say to someone close to you, "I never want to come to the place where I don't *appreciate* your approval, but I do want to come to the place where I don't *need* it for survival." You will know you are growing when you weigh the expectations of people and then do what you believe is best. Here are some further indicators of growth for an *adaptive* personality.

I know I am growing when:
- I understand that it is more important how conflict is handled than that conflict takes place.
- I realize that I am the key to my personal success and security.
- I buy the car that best meets my needs whether or not it's the "latest."
- I am more concerned with doing what's best for someone, whether or not they like me.

Here is a brief summary of the five types, their needs, and fears:

TYPE	NEED	FEAR
Apathetic	Not to be involved, responsible, or committed	Involvement
Aggressive	Security, Control, Power	Loss of perceived or real power
Analytical	Details, Exactness	Ambiguity
Adaptive	Recognition, Compatibility	Rejection, Discord
Self-Actualized	To develop, grow, create	None

When you understand the needs of the personality types, you can focus on meeting those needs, knowing that in doing so you can eliminate the fear and that will allow you to build a relationship of trust.

Here is a practical application of this information for a selling situation. As a seller of real estate, you have gone through the four questions with a potential client and determined that you have an *aggressive* client. Their need in a house is that it be well built. Strong and secure. Concrete floors, and a big yard—with a fence. If it has a swimming pool you might talk about the opportunity of doing some laps.

These types are difficult to sell life insurance to, because they believe they will live forever. They have been known to work all day with a 102° fever, denying they are sick. In automobiles, they're interested in horsepower.

Here is what might happen if you were showing a house to an *analytical* engineer and were not aware of his need. As you walked into the first house, he might ask you, "How big is this living room?" If your reply were, "Well, my best *guess* is that it's *about* . . ." you probably just lost the sale. Your best answer would sound something like, "According to my *calculations,* this room is *exactly* fourteen feet six inches by sixteen feet eight inches." Now you're meeting his needs and he loves it! If he is interested in buying an automobile, you sell him the intricate designs of engineering.

When contracts are to be signed, make sure that every space is filled in. Don't skip a thing. If at all possible, have them typed, neat and clean. If all the details are there, it will help allay his suspicions.

With an *adaptive* client, it's primarily what's popular. What's in? With clothing it's the vogue and fashionable. With real estate, "your kind of people live around here." It's often referred to as "curb appeal." If their friends recommended it, the deal is practically closed in advance.

Since Maslow informed us that there were so few *self-actualizers,* we probably won't be dealing with many of them. In buying anything, their basic determining factors are: Is it valuable? Do I need it? Is it wise?

Knowing that the desire of a great lover is to continue the process of growth, here are some of the characteristics of the self-actualizing personality. This will give us an ideal to visualize. I would suggest that you spend a lot of time thinking about these attributes and even make them into some personal affirmations for the feeding of your subconscious mind.

> Childlike simplicity and lack of arrogance. Balanced between their "child" and "parent." Ability to listen to others, and admit they don't know everything. Finds happiness in helping others. Enjoys play. Enjoys work. Work becomes play. Spontaneous. Acceptance of others cuts across political, economic, and national boundaries. Tolerant of others' shortcomings. Intolerant about dishonesty, lying, cheating, cruelty, and hypocrisy. They have a sense of humor, but not of the ordinary type; they do not laugh at humor which ridicules people or makes someone else appear inferior. The more mature they become, the less attracted they are by such characteristics as handsome, good-looking, good dancer, physically strong, tall, handsome body, good necker, and the more they speak of compatibility, goodness, decency, good companionship, considerateness. They have the capacity to appreciate the sunrise again and again and again.[2]

The self-actualizer loves life. He is a great lover. He has beaten the system!

Step Ten to Becoming a Great Lover: I will help others to live without fear by being aware of and sensitive to their needs.

Workshop:

1. What four questions help to identify people's needs?
2. With which personality type do you most closely identify?
3. Make personal affirmation cards from the list of characteristics of the self-actualized personality. Begin to read and visualize them each day.

---

2. Ibid. Taken randomly from chapter 3.

Unit IV

Where Love Can Take Us

- "I Can Hardly Wait"

- You've Got What It Takes

11

"I Can Hardly Wait"

When my children were little, their attitudes reminded me of one of life's most exciting motivators. It is a major key to accomplishment and successful living. It is a priceless tool that is available to anyone who wants to use it. It is the power of anticipation.

One day I was suddenly aware that their lives were full of "I can hardly waits." They could hardly wait for dessert, they could hardly wait until Saturday, they could hardly wait until the new baby arrived. They had a number of "I can hardly waits" spread over a period of weeks, all going simultaneously! That's motivation! Simone and I had difficulty convincing them to go to bed at night, but we never had trouble getting them up in the morning. It seemed that every day was the source of some new excitement, and their enthusiasm stimulated each other and rubbed off on me.

When children lose their sense of "I can hardly wait," what do they become? Adults who suffer from boredom. They may be busy adults, but they're bored because they have nothing to look forward to—no purpose. Boredom brings more problems than distress does.

Purpose—The Great Motivator

Purpose is what drives us in life. Purpose motivates us and gives meaning to what we do. Without purpose, we're like the man who was digging a ditch. Somebody stopped him and asked, "Why are you digging that ditch?"

"I've got to have money."

145

"Why do you need money?"
"To buy food."
"Why do you need food?"
"For strength."
"Why do you need strength?"
"So I can dig ditches."

That kind of existence isn't *life;* it's a vicious circle. What about you? Would you do what you do if you weren't being paid for it? If not, it's just a job. Without purpose, life has no meaning.

So many people today are complaining of the feeling of total and ultimate meaninglessness in their lives. They lack the awareness of something worth living for. They are haunted by the experience of their inner emptiness, a void within their circle. They seem to be caught up in a spiritual vacuum.

The Freudian school seemed to believe that man's primary motivational force was the pleasure principle or the *will to pleasure.* Adlerian psychology stressed the power principle or the *will to power.* In contrast to this, Dr. Viktor Frankl in his concepts of logotherapy believed that the primary motivational force in man's life was a striving for meaning or purpose or the *will to meaning.* Logotherapy is less *retrospective* and *introspective* and focuses rather on the future, that is to say, on the assignments and meanings that I am to fulfill in life. How do I find the meaning and purpose of my life?

Each of us must discover his own specific vocation or mission in life. Each of us has a definite assignment that demands fulfillment. Each of our tasks is as unique as our specific opportunity to implement it. Therefore, we cannot be replaced, nor can our lives be repeated! Each of us is questioned by life, and we can only answer to life by answering for our *own* life, and we can only respond to life by being responsible.

Much of Frankl's logotherapy was developed from his experiences and observations as a prisoner in a Nazi war camp. It is spoken of in his book, *Man's Search For Meaning.* In trying to determine why some people survived in the camps while most perished, he made an interesting observation: The survivors always seemed to have a purpose for living—even if the purpose was to record the events so that history would not repeat itself. Often it was a sense of being needed that kept them going.

But this was not true of those who had no purpose, nothing to look forward to, no sense of being needed. Frankl watched them die daily. They curled up like animals and gave up. The prisoners who had lost faith in the future—their own future—were doomed. It is a peculiarity of man that he can only live by looking into the future . . . when he has hope, when he has some "I can hardly waits"!

Everyone Needs a Vision

The wise man of Proverbs wrote: "Where there is no vision, the people perish. . . ."[1]

Do you have a vision—a plan, a dream, a purpose? What is your ultimate goal? What is the final benefit you hope to experience or gain in life? Do your dreams outweigh your memories? Do you know the magic of "I can hardly wait"? Where do you plan to be five years from now? What do you plan to be doing?

The most common answer to that last question is "Oh, probably the same old thing." If that is your answer, I can guarantee that you won't be disappointed. Why? Because you've planned it by default. It's like the book I remember reading entitled *If You Don't Know Where You're Going, You'll Probably End Up Someplace Else.*

Before we talk about setting goals for our lives, it is important that we have worked through the process of love and fear, of love and performance, of self-esteem and self-worth. How can "unworthy" people set worthy goals? Now we can emphasize that productive achievement is a *consequence* and an *expression* of

---

1. Proverbs 29:18.

healthy self-esteem. A person who feels unfit for existence is incapable of enjoying life. One of the characteristics of self-esteem is a person's eagerness for the new and challenging—the desire to go for it! The primary desire of the person lacking in self-confidence is to be "safe."

I PURSUE EXCELLENCE
THE TRUE, THE GOOD, THE BEAUTIFUL

Before we can establish our goals, we need to examine our values and determine our priorities. Then we can make realistic plans that reflect our genuine desires, motives, and purposes. To do this, let's begin by taking a simple inventory of some of our values.

Let's look at the five general areas of life with this definition of success: **Success is the ability to build and maintain physical, intellectual, spiritual, social, and financial equity.**

Physical	Intellectual	Spiritual	Social Relational	Financial Vocational

Figure 9.

Looking at these five areas and considering equity, prosperity, and health as being over and against poverty and unhealthiness, which area do you consider to be:

The Most Important＿＿＿＿＿＿＿＿＿＿＿＿＿＿＿＿

The Least Important＿＿＿＿＿＿＿＿＿＿＿＿＿＿＿＿

The Hardest in Which to Attain Equity＿＿＿＿＿＿＿＿

The Easiest in Which to Attain Equity＿＿＿＿＿＿＿＿

After you have done the above, we can get another perspective on our values and their impact on our lives by thinking of the five areas as two concentric circles. The inner circle represents the dimension we consider to be most important, while the outer circle contains the four other areas. In Figure 10, I have put the Spiritual–Psychological in the inner circle as my personal preference. In Figure 11 fill in the concentric circles so they reflect your own priorities.

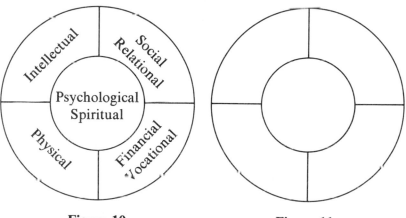

Figure 10.   **Figure 11.**

Our Attitudes Toward Money

In many cases, the people who participate in my seminars place Vocational–Financial equity in the center circle. For this reason, I want to spend some time considering our attitudes toward money. I can't offer answers to the questions about money, but perhaps together we can probe your views and put them into perspective.

When we talked about living from the inside out, we learned that money is outside the circle, and that the responsibility and control of our lives is inside the circle. We also learned that we are responsible for our own feelings. We can choose to allow our attitudes about money to control us, or we can control our attitudes about money.

Spending. There are three areas in which our feelings about money affect our choices and goals and our purpose. The first area is our attitude toward *spending.* When we make price the deciding factor we are allowing money to control us. To test this, think about whether you could go through just one day and make every decision you need to make and not once refer to money.

It's much like the childhood game many of us played called Mother, May I? You had to ask permission to take a giant step, or a scissor step, or a baby step. And if you failed to ask, "Mother, May I?" you had to go back and start all over.

Most of us still play that game every day. All we've done is change the word from *mother* to *dollar.* All day long it sounds like "Dollar, May I?" And what's the usual answer?

There is a way to keep price from being the deciding factor. Suppose I knocked on your front door and attempted to sell you a glass of water for two dollars. It's good water. It's pure and refreshing. The glass is clean. Would you buy it? Probably not. Why?

You don't *need* that glass of water. You already have all you need in your own kitchen, and it would not be *wise* to spend your money for that item. It is not *worth* two dollars, the *value* is not there. Is the price the issue? No. It wouldn't matter if the price were two dollars or two cents.

Now let me find you out in the desert after three days without any supplies and offer you the same glass of water. Is it valuable? Do you need it? Would it be a wise investment? Is price the issue? No. Whether here today or in the desert next week, the price would not be the issue. To keep cost from being the deciding factor, learn to ask these three questions—

DO I NEED IT?

IS IT VALUABLE?

IS IT WISE?

"Is it wise?" is probably the most important question.

Earning. The second view is our attitude toward how much we *earn.* How much money did *you* earn last year? Chances are—and you may not like this—whether you earned three dollars per hour or fifty thousand dollars a year, you probably earned what you think you deserved or were worth. If you had earned any more, you would probably have had difficulty dealing with it. Psychologically, it is difficult for us to receive what we don't feel we deserve. Consequently, we set limits in terms of what we think we're worth.

There is a story about a man who had all the qualifications of a fantastic salesman. Management brought him in, trained him, and put him in their very best territory. The first year he made seven thousand dollars, but it was a twenty-thousand-dollar territory.

Management took him out and put him in their worst territory. That year he earned seven thousand dollars again. Impressed that the salesman had learned to do better, management returned him to the best territory. Again he earned seven thousand dollars. He saw himself as a seven-thousand-dollar-a-year salesman, and he couldn't rise above his self-image.

Only rarely do I have an opportunity to do seminars for people who receive hourly or weekly wages. On one recent occasion, I was talking to some of these people about how to make more money. At the coffee break a woman approached me and with a little anger in her voice said, "David, you're being unfair. You talk primarily to management and salespeople who receive commissions and bonuses, and for them, income is open-ended. But we're on fixed salaries and you're telling us how to make more money. It's not fair!"

I replied, "Do you have any idea how many salespeople are on a fixed salary? All of them," I told her. And it wasn't set by the union, the government, or management. We all set our own salaries. We set our own limits of income.

Of course, our worth has nothing to do with our wages. As persons we have infinite value no matter what we earn. But there is a correlation between our self-concept, what we feel we deserve, and what we are able to receive. This can best be seen in what some believe to be our most common fear: the fear of success. The fear of success is *not* getting what you really want because you *unconsciously* feel you don't deserve it.

The fear of success seems to be a paradox. On a conscious level, no one is afraid of success; everyone wants to be successful. But on an unconscious level, in that place few of us ever really explore, it's often quite a different story. There, in the unconscious, is where many of us do our best, without realizing it, to ensure that success is never attained or, if it is, that it doesn't last.

Several years ago a man canceled an appointment with me, with the explanation that his best friend's wife, aged twenty-eight, had just taken her own life. He said that she left a four-line message behind: "I'm too happy. I don't deserve it. It can't last. I'm quitting while I'm ahead."

Have you ever knocked on wood? Have you ever said, "That's too good to be true" or "That's too good to last." Do you know what you're really saying?

When one's self-image does not match one's accomplishments, the fear of success will dominate and undermine it.

There is a man in Los Angeles who gives seminars just for people who have inherited great sums of money, a minimum of $300,000. These people need help simply to adjust to having received something they didn't deserve or earn. Those who can't deal with that will blow it. That's why some people who have inherited wealth go into public service or politics. They feel a need to deserve it and earn it *after the fact*. And, if they don't do something to deserve it and earn it, they often have a difficult time handling it.

There is an interesting correlation between love and money in that they both seem difficult for us to receive if we feel we have not earned it, are not qualified for it, or do not deserve it.

Giving. The third area in which our attitudes about money affect our choices and goals and purpose is our attitude of *giving.* Most people seem to think of life in terms of getting and taking, first, and then consider a contribution. They have the attitude that "as soon as I get some heat out of that stove, I'll put some wood in it." For everyone, great lovers and otherwise, life is a matter of understanding the law of sowing and reaping.

> . . . He which sows sparingly shall reap also sparingly; and he who sows bountifully shall reap also bountifully. Every man according as he purposes in his heart, so let him give; not grudgingly, or of necessity: for God loves a cheerful giver![2]
>
> Give, and gifts will be given you. Good measure, pressed down, shaken together, and running over, will be poured into your lap; for whatever measure you deal out to others will be dealt to you in return.[3]

The thought of lack attracts poverty. The thought of destitution attracts lack. Thoughts of having nothing become self-fulfilling prophecies.

Love gives from its unlimited resources. Love is a spendthrift. No one is too poor to give; he is too poor *not* to give. The principle of giving will either break the spirit of poverty in your life if you think you are poor, or it will break your bondage to things, if you are wealthy.

A generous giver is also a gracious receiver. Several years ago my daughter, Brenda, came to me with a beautifully wrapped package. She had wrapped it as only a child can—with about two

---

2. *See* 2 Corinthians 9:6, 7.
3. Luke 6:38 NEB.

rolls of cellophane tape. She wanted me to have this item for my desk. When I finally got it open, I discovered it was just a plain, old, everyday California redwood chip. She wanted me to have it as a paperweight for the papers on my desk. Now, quite frankly, I believe that I *deserve* a redwood chip. It was very easy for me to receive it.

But what if Brenda had saved her allowance for a whole year and bought me a gold-plated paperweight? Could I have received that gold-plated weight as easily as I did the redwood chip? Why not? Isn't it the thought that counts? (I wonder why we always say that when it's cheap. I've never known anyone to give an expensive gift and say, "It's the thought that counts.") It *is* the thought that counts, but there is something in me that says, *Hey, you shouldn't have done that. I don't deserve it.*

There's another side to this issue, and that is what I would have done to that child by saying I don't deserve it. I would also be saying, "You have poor judgment." Who am I to decide what she should give! That child has a need to give; and if somebody doesn't receive, her need can't be met. So I can be loving and gracious and say, "Thank you very much," or I can be selfish and say, "You shouldn't have done it."

Early on, we can teach our children a healthy, balanced attitude toward money. If we give them an allowance no matter what they do, they begin to develop a "welfare" mentality. If we feel they should earn every penny, they will have a difficult time experiencing grace, that is, receiving something good that they don't deserve. The balance can be achieved by sometimes withholding an allowance which isn't earned and by sometimes giving them something "for no good reason."

Money—The Root of All Evil?

Of course, we can't leave this subject until we've talked about the love of money and the root of all evil. I'm sure you have heard people say that money is the root of all evil. My experience has been that those who *say* that ain't got any! They're trying to convince you that there is virtue in poverty. Money is *not* the root of evil. It's our attitude toward the commodity that makes it what it is—just like everything else outside our circle.

As far as I know, at this moment you are not worried about whether you've got enough oxygen to last until the end of the month. You are just sitting there breathing. Just taking it in and letting it out. You're relaxed. You weren't even thinking about oxygen until I mentioned it.

You're not worried about your neighbors being greedy and getting more than their share. If a new person comes into your area, you won't panic, thinking to yourself, *Here comes another one. I'd better get a little extra!* As long as you believe there is plenty, you're relaxed.

But what if you were out in the ocean, scuba diving, and your tank was running out of air, what would preoccupy you? Getting air! What would you do to get it? Whatever it takes! And do you know what that proves? The love of oxygen is the root of all evil. Who "loves" oxygen the most? The one who is preoccupied with getting it because he is convinced there is not enough. Now you know about the love of money.

Truly Successful Living

In light of all this, let's go back to the definition of success which dealt with the five areas of our life. Now we are in a better position to treat the financial dimension as an effect rather than as a cause and attain more balance in our lives.

True success is to be prosperous in all five areas. Successful living is to be a whole person. It's for this reason that I believe that the most important area of the five is the psychological–spiritual. It is also the most difficult in which to be prosperous and healthy. And that's what this book has been all about.

> Beloved, I wish above all things that you may *prosper* and be in *good health,* even as your *soul prospers.*[4]

---

4. *See* 3 John 2.

Consider what happens to your body, for example, when you are not emotionally healthy. We've already discussed the fact that a very high percentage of our physical problems are emotionally induced. The lack of emotional health and strength can have a devastating impact on our physical lives.

The relationship between our psychological health and mental acumen is also astounding. Often when a child is doing badly in school, it can be traced to his feeling badly about himself—low self-esteem. More often than not, you can solve the problem by concentrating on raising the child's self-esteem, rather than pressuring him for better grades.

I think it is obvious that there is a link between our psychological health and our ability to "win friends and influence people." If it's true that we love our neighbor as we love ourselves, I know a lot of neighbors who are in trouble. We can only accept and feel good about others as we are able to accept and feel good about ourselves.

Finally, I think the relationship between our spiritual prosperity and our financial prosperity is much closer than most of us are even aware of or willing to admit. There is a direct corollary between the prosperity of our spirit and the prosperity of every other dimension of our lives. If I have love in my life, it can make up for a great many "things" I lack. If I do not have love, no matter what else there is, it is not enough. Someone has described the materialism of our day (which is not synonymous with prosperity) as the "fig leaves to cover the nakedness of an insecure life."

It is easy to talk about goal setting, about things we want to do, about making money, about making friends, to talk about being wiser and having healthy bodies, but completely ignore that which makes it possible.

The future of our lives is not going to be determined by economic circumstances or situations but by purpose. Successful, loving people have a strong purpose and the strength that holds them to their purpose is not their own strength, but the strength of the purpose itself. We can never succeed beyond the purpose to which we are willing to give ourselves.

It's easier to adjust ourselves to the hardships of a poor living than it is to adjust ourselves to the hardships of making a better one. But let's go for it in the next chapter. I don't know about you—but I can hardly wait!

Step Eleven to Becoming a Great Lover: I realize that my ultimate purpose is not happiness or personal fulfillment, but the power and freedom to give myself sacrificially.

Workshop:

1. Go to the Self-Esteem Exercise and check your answers to questions 19, 22, 23, 31, 33, 42, and 48.
2. What are the three questions we can ask to keep money from being the deciding factor?
3. Where is the focus of your life right now? Past, present, or future?
4. Which of the five areas of your life need the most attention at this time?
5. Why is the psychological–spiritual more important than the others?
6. What is the result of not having any "I can hardly waits"?
7. What is behind the fear of success? How can the fear be eliminated?

12

You've Got What It Takes

If one advances confidently in the direction of his dreams, and en-deavors to live the life which he has imagined, he will meet with a success unexpected in common hours.

HENRY DAVID THOREAU

If we are going to "advance confidently" in the direction of *our* dreams, we are going to need a plan. We make plans for relatively simple aspects of our lives, such as vacations. We decide where to go, how far to drive, where to stop, and how long it will take. But when it comes to life, most of us just take it as it comes—one day at a time, so far, so good.

That attitude reminds me of the man who fell off the fourteenth floor of a building. As he passed each floor, someone heard him say, "So far, so good!" You might call that positive thinking, but it is not very creative. When people lack creativity and planning, they come to the end of their lives and wonder why they have nothing to show for all their years of effort. Yet there is no virtue in working hard if you don't accomplish what you want to do.

There is another side to the goal-setting coin. Creativity alone is not enough. We all know dreamers who constantly have new ideas. They have million-dollar dreams and enough enthusiasm to move heaven and earth—but nothing happens. They forget one necessary ingredient: We have to do something *today* if we are going to fulfill our dreams for *tomorrow*.

In the remaining pages of this book we are going to do some of the preliminary work that will make things happen for us. To begin, we will reexamine each of the five areas of our lives: the social–relational, the physical, the financial–vocational, the intellectual, and the psychological–spiritual. On a scale of one to ten—one being needy and ten being prosperous—where do you think you are in each category?

On the Goal-Setting Chart (Figure 12), record your estimate in the box with a line (see example). If you are sluggish and overweight, or if you are ill more often than not, you may decide to draw a line at 2 in the physical box. If you play raquetball three times a week and drink carrot juice daily, you may decide you are a physical 9. Let me suggest that no one is a 10, because that would mean there is absolutely no room for growth and improvement.

Next, draw a broken line at the number you would *like* to be in each category (see example). Maybe you would like to go from a 5 to a 6 intellectually. Perhaps you are a 7 financially, and you feel content with that. Again, avoid marking a 10 because it is unrealistic. No matter how hard you try, perfection will always be out of reach.

Now that you've decided where you *are* (5) and where you would *like to be* (7), let's determine what it will take to get you there. In each of the five areas we want to establish a *long*-range

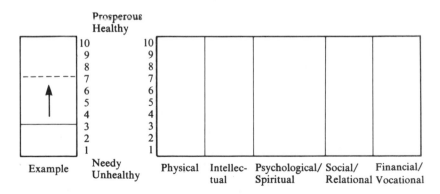

Figure 12.

goal (more than six months away), and a *short*-range goal (immediate action). It will look like this:

PHYSICAL
(Example)
      Long-range goal: Lose 25 pounds
      Short-range goal: One small serving at dinner and no snacks

Now fill in your own:
      Long-range goal: _____
      Short-range goal: _____

INTELLECTUAL
(Example)
      Long-range goal: Read 18 books this coming year
      Short-range goal: Read 15 minutes every day

Now fill in your own:
      Long-range goal: _____
      Short-range goal: _____

PSYCHOLOGICAL–SPIRITUAL
(Example)
      Long-range goal: Live without fear
      Short-range goal: Do something loving every day

Now fill in your own:
      Long-range goal: _____
      Short-range goal: _____

SOCIAL–RELATIONAL
(Example)
      Long-range goal: Spend a week in Tahiti
      Short-range goal: Set the date and open a special savings
      account

Now fill in your own:
      Long-range goal: _____
      Short-range goal: _____

FINANCIAL–VOCATIONAL
(Example)
Long-range goal: Be the head of my division in the company
Short-range goal: Find out requirements and *act as if* I already was

Now fill in your own:
Long-range goal:
Short-range goal:

Because most long-range goals overwhelm us and discourage us, we need to break them down into manageable segments. Reading eighteen books in one year may seem like an insurmountable task, for example, but anyone can read fifteen minutes a day. Losing twenty-five pounds in one year may seem like an impossible dream, but anyone can manage to lose eight ounces each week. These easily handled fractions of the long-range goals become our short-range goals. Decide what your short-range goals are going to be. Be specific. Then record your goals for each area.

Our next task is an important part of setting goals. It is the matter of counting the cost. No matter what choices we make in life, there is a price to pay. As someone has said, "If you think that education is expensive, try ignorance." You will pay the price for good health or the price for poor health. You will pay the price for success or the price for failure. You will pay the price for working on your marriage or you will pay the price for neglecting your marriage. You will pay the price for love or you will pay the price for fear.

Sometimes our choices are costly in terms of dollars, and other times they are costly because of the many hours needed for their pursuit. Sometimes the cost is extensive physical effort, and other times our relationships pay the price.

To reach our goals in each of the five areas, what will it cost in time? How many hours? How many days? If your social–relational goal is to stop working a twelve-hour day so that you can spend more time with your family, what will the financial consequences be?

What about the energy you spend? Will you have to lose any sleep? If you want to go to night school, will you have enough energy after working an eight-hour day? Will a ten-hour work day rob you of planting a garden and smelling the flowers?

In the spaces below, try to determine the costs of your goals in each of the five areas. Record the costs in terms of time, money, energy, and relationships.

Example
INTELLECTUAL (Read 18 books in a year)

TIME   15 minutes per day
ENERGY   very little
MONEY $18 per month
(18 books at $12 each)
RELATIONSHIPS   no cost

PHYSICAL

TIME_____
ENERGY_____ (A lot or little)
MONEY_____
RELATIONSHIPS_____

INTELLECTUAL

TIME_____
ENERGY_____
MONEY_____
RELATIONSHIPS_____

PSYCHOLOGICAL

TIME_____
ENERGY_____
MONEY_____
RELATIONSHIPS_____

SOCIAL

> TIME_____
> ENERGY_____
> MONEY_____
> RELATIONSHIPS_____

FINANCIAL

> TIME_____
> ENERGY_____
> MONEY_____
> RELATIONSHIPS_____

After you have determined the costs of reaching your goals in each of these areas, ask yourself the question, *Am I willing to pay the price? Yes or No?*

This is where a lot of people drop out of the ballgame. They say they want to achieve certain things, but when you get down to what it will take, they seem to lose interest. Someone will say, "I'd like to be healthy, but I hate to exercise and I don't want to give up smoking." This decision is, of course, determined by their values.

On the other hand, there are those who are willing to pay too high a price. They want what they want so much that they are willing to make any sacrifice to get it, and they are hurting themselves and others in the long run.

I presented a seminar at an insurance company not too long ago, and I met a woman who had been with the company for only four years. This is a relatively short time in the insurance business, but she was already number five in the company.

More than anything else, she wanted to be number one. Her desire and her efforts to reach her goal had already cost her a marriage. At the time I met her, she was beginning to lose touch with her children. She was having to decide, *Is it worth it? What are my priorities?* I haven't seen her since then, but from what she shared with me, I believe she is probably number one by now—and very lonely.

I PURSUE EXCELLENCE
WITH BALANCE AND COMPASSION

I'm not saying that it has to be that way, but too often it is. We live in a materialistic, consumer-oriented system that keeps telling us we need more money, more power, more everything in order to be happy and satisfied. They continually stir up discontent by reminding people of all the things they *don't* have. (If you don't have a trash compactor you're still living in the dark ages!)

What they won't tell us is, we also have to count the cost. How will our efforts to obtain our goals affect our mate, our children, our friends? It may not cost us anything, but on the other hand, the price might be too high.

CONTENTMENT IS THE REALIZATION
OF HOW MUCH I ALREADY HAVE

The final phase in making things happen for ourselves can be summarized in five words. With these five things—**visualization, belief, desire, action, commitment**—working for you, I would like to prove once and for all that

YOU'VE GOT WHAT IT TAKES!

The first thing we have to make things happen is **visualization** or imagination. Imagination is something that we all have. The only consideration is whether we use it positively or negatively; but use it we will. Flip Wilson used to remind us that "What you see is what you get." But that's not imagination. Imagination is what you "see" with your eyes *closed;* which is ten thousand times more than we can see with our eyes open.

Has anyone ever suggested that you try something and your response was, "Wow, I can never see myself doing anything like that." And you're probably right. If you can't "see" yourself doing it, you probably won't be able to achieve it.

From the word *imagination* we hear terms like "imaging" and "guided imagery." O. Carl Simonton, M.D., is known for his use of guided imagery, along with meditation and some chemotherapy in the remission and healing of cancer in some patients. Part of the healing process was to "see" the cancer being devoured by good cells.

Dr. Norman Vincent Peale has written a book called *Positive Imaging.* In it he tells us, "Imaging, the forming of mental pictures or images, is based on the principle that there is a deep tendency in human nature to ultimately become precisely like that which we imagine or image ourselves as being. An image formed and held tenaciously in the conscious mind will pass presently, by a process of mental osmosis, into the unconscious mind. And when it is accepted firmly in the unconscious, the individual will strongly tend to have it, for then it has you. So powerful is the imaging effect on thought and performance that a long-held visualization of an objective or goal can become determinative."

To prove that you are creative in your imagination, let's look at a very common negative phenomenon. Do you ever worry? How much do you worry? How often? What is the process when you are worrying? Creative! You are creating something out of nothing! It's all negative—below the line—but it is still something out of nothing.

The worrying proves two things: (1) that you're creative and (2) that you have low self-esteem. The object of this book has been to help you raise your self-esteem so that you can use your creativity, *positively.* You've got what it takes; it's just a matter of how you use it—and self-esteem is the difference.

Most of us have experienced saying things to ourselves, like, *That's sure a dumb idea,* or *I had an idea, but I doubt if it's worth mentioning.* I want to remind you of a story that might help stop this habit and at the same time keep you awake a few nights. This person decided to collect some ordinary rocks, to clean them, and polish them, and to pack them in small boxes with excelsior in the bottom so they could be comfortable.

Next he poked little holes in the sides of the boxes so the rocks could get fresh air—and he called them "Pet Rocks." Now who in the world would be willing to pay ten dollars for a Pet Rock—let alone ten dollars to have it cremated? Somebody made a lot of money on a "dumb" idea. Now I'm hoping that this little story will keep you awake at night wondering about all of the "dumb" million-dollar ideas that you may have flushed.

Stop evaluating your ideas. Acknowledge them. Let them grow. Let your imagination create positive things for you. It will, if you don't get in its way. Whatever the mind can conceive (imagine) and believe, it can achieve.

The second thing that we have that makes things happen is **belief.** Again, there is no question as to whether or not you have any belief, or faith. The only question is, is your belief positive or negative? We've talked a lot about love and shared several definitions. We've also talked about fear, but I haven't given you a definition. Now I want to give you one:

FEAR IS NEGATIVE FAITH

Just as worry proves that you're a creative genius, every time you're fearful it proves you have enormous faith—but it's negative and destructive. Raising your self-esteem and self-worth will change your faith from negative and destructive to positive and productive.

I've had people say to me, "David, I don't accept your ideas on goal setting. I tried it once. I wrote down some six-month goals and I tried real hard. I desired them, I visualized them; I did everything I could to make them happen. Six months came and six months went, and nothing happened—and I knew it wouldn't."

What did they have operating for six months? Negative faith. And what happened? Exactly what they believed would happen. Do you remember what Job said? "For the thing which I greatly feared is come upon me, and that which I was afraid of is come unto me."[1]

The chances are that the minute you start writing some goals down and start taking some risks, that little voice in the back of your mind is going to start talking to you and it will sound rather familiar: *Who do you think you are? You can't do that! What are people going to think? You're going to make a fool out of yourself! You're going to be sorry. You're setting yourself up for disappointment.* And what are you likely to start believing? Everything that little voice is telling you. And what do you think is going to happen? *Everything that you believe.*

If you really want to find out what you believe, try this: Tell me what surprises you, and I'll tell you what you believe.

When something good happens to most people, what's their response? "Unbelievable" or, "Absolutely incredible" or, "Man, was I lucky; that'll never happen to me again in a million years." They are surprised when something good happens.

Then, when something bad happens, what's the response? "I knew it." "It figures." "Why me again?"

There are very few surprises in life. I really believe that we are going to get out of life mainly what we expect and anticipate. With low self-esteem we are afraid to expect the good for fear of disappointment. I've discovered that those who fear the worst are seldom disappointed. Tell me what surprises you, and I'll tell you what you believe.

Some time ago I listened in on a conversation between a doctor and several sets of parents who had children with mental retardation. The doctor was trying to encourage the parents regarding the future of their youngsters. "It would be better for you," he

---

1. Job 3:25

said, "to aim toward the university and miss it, than to aim toward the institution and hit it."

One of the worst things in selling is to tell a salesperson that the
closing quotient is about one out of seven. What are they going to
believe about the first six? They don't want to bother with them
and a lot of potential customers get skipped. Somebody who
doesn't know there's a quota might sell three out of seven.

If you're a salesperson, I wonder if you're ever surprised when
you close a sale. You better not be. What does that say you were
expecting? That you believed you wouldn't get it. It sounds like,
"I just knew they wouldn't buy." It's better to be surprised when
you *don't* close a sale. "I can't believe it. They really didn't buy.
Have *they* got a problem?"

Gratitude Prior to Reception

The problem is not that we aim too high and miss; the problem
is that we aim too low and hit. Raise your sights! Expect the best
and risk a few disappointments! Keep the faith! Gratitude *prior* to
reception is a spiritual law that guarantees results!

After visualization and belief comes **desire.** How much do you
really want to attain your goals? If it's a "take it or leave it"
attitude, the odds are that you will leave it. How badly do you
want it?

One evening after a concert, a lady walked up to the pianist
and said, "I'd give my life to play the piano like that." "That's
what it cost me; my life," he replied. That's desire.

A story about Alexander the Great gives us an idea of how desire can develop. On one of his many conquests, he developed a
tactic that one might call "do or die." After his men had gone
ashore, Alexander had all of *his own boats* sunk in the harbor.

As his men were storming the beachhead, they received this
message: "If and when we go home, we'll go home in the *enemy's*
boats!" Can you imagine those men saying, "Well, let's give it a
try!" It is absolutely amazing what we can accomplish when we
have no options.

A young man walked up to an old philosopher one day and asked, "What do I have to do to find the truth?"

"How badly do you really want to know?" asked the philosopher.

"I *really* desire to know the truth," the young man replied.

"Very well," the philosopher said, "come with me." Together they walked in silence until they reached the ocean. The old man beckoned the young man to go with him into the water. Then, without warning, the old man grabbed the young seeker of truth by the shoulders and shoved him under the water.

The boy kicked and thrashed and sputtered for what seemed like an eternity. Finally he was released, and he popped to the surface, gasping for air.

"You're crazy!" he shouted when he caught his breath. "I asked you to help me find the truth, and you nearly drowned me. What are you trying to do?"

"Teach you a lesson," he replied. "Young man, when you want truth as much as you wanted air—you'll find it." That's desire.

How much do you want to reach your goal? Desire is more than wishful thinking. Wishful thinking sounds like desire, but it's negative. It always ends with a "but." "I wish I could do that, *but* I probably can't make it." Desire is like a strong magnet pulling you toward your goal.

The fourth necessity is **action**. Whatever the mind can conceive and believe it can *achieve*. Action is almost automatic. Action is the result of vivid imagination, strong belief, and burning desire. Let's see how this might take place.

What if your long-range social goal were to take your spouse or a friend to Tahiti next year? That's a long time away—but what could you do within the next few days to make it start to happen. First, you could agree that it was a desirable goal. Together you could check the calendar and circle the date you want.

Then you could go down to the local travel agency and pick up all the folders and brochures they have about Tahiti. (Looking at all of those pictures will help your imagination and desire!) Then you give the travel agent a *nonrefundable deposit*. Now I want you to check in on your reaction to that "nonrefundable deposit," because I've just tapped into your faith. If your faith is negative, your response was, "hold on just a minute! I don't want to go *that* far with this. Who knows what could happen in the next year?" See how your imagination works.

Or, if your faith is positive, your response was, "Hey, that's a great idea. That's one way to make sure it will happen."

What I've done here without mentioning it, is ask you for the fifth requirement: **commitment.** I asked you to make a commitment, and if your faith was negative, I got a fear response. Commitment seals the decision and that can be scary for some. Commitment is the completion of the statement in the Self-Esteem Exercise, "I can do almost anything I really *set my mind to.*" Commitment is a way of "sinking your own boats in the harbor."

You might be asking, "Will you guarantee me that if I visualize and believe and desire and make a commitment, something will happen?" No, I won't. I will guarantee you this: If you *don't* visualize your goals, believe them, desire them and make a commitment—*nothing* will happen.

All through this book, I've been giving some positive affirmations along the way to help strengthen the ideas that I've wanted to leave with you. What can be very exciting is to experience your children responding to them.

We have a very long, narrow yard in the front of our house. Kevin likes to hit the baseball to me and as long as he hits it the "long" way there is no problem. On a recent evening, after hitting the ball to me several times, we had to go into the house for dinner. As we were going in, Kevin said, "I want to hit the ball over the house." Now that could have been a problem. We were standing about fifteen feet from the house and it's fairly high.

I said, "Kevin, that's too risky. You're too close." He said, "I can do it." I replied, "If you knock out a window it may cost you a month's allowance." He looked me straight in the eye and said, "Progress Always Involves Risk!" Pow! He knocked it over the house.

When my second daughter, Julene, was in the fourth grade, the class was given an assignment to answer a letter as if they were an Ann Landers type of columnist. Here is the letter they were given and Julene's reply.

Dear Aunt Lucy:
 I have a sister who is pretty and one who is very smart. I have a brother who is so witty that people laugh the minute he opens his mouth.
 People look at me as if I've got nothing. I'm beginning to think they are right. I feel dumb, ugly, and sour most of the time. What can I do about myself? Please hurry with your answer. I need your help.

Sincerely,
Miss Nobody

Julene's reply was: "If you're loved, that's all that matters." I hope she remembers that. I hope I remember that. I hope you remember that. Because she's right! If you're loved that's all that matters. And you are.

I AM LOVED
I AM ACCEPTED
I AM FORGIVEN
I AM FREE

Step Twelve to Becoming a Great Lover: I am loved, accepted, forgiven, and free. I know I have what it takes to be a Great Lover.

APPENDIX

The following pages contain exercises and additional information that you may find useful as you practice the principles of how to be a Great Lover of people and experience *The Ultimate Power*. They include—

Values Inventory
Interpretation of Values Inventory
Instructions for Taking Self-Esteem Exercise
Self-Esteem Exercise
Scoring Sheet for Self-Esteem Exercise
Interpretation of Self-Esteem Exercise
Growth Inhibitors
Checkpoints for Growth
The Great Lover's Manifesto

VALUES INVENTORY

(Use a separate piece of paper to record your answers.)

1. What do you want *most* out of life? (Limit to five items.)
2. Describe yourself in twenty-five words or less. Your personality, your character, your mind, your social life, and so on.
3. Complete this statement, made by your best friend: "He or she is a great human being, but . . ."
4. Out of all of your assets and strengths, what do you like best about yourself?
5. What is the finest compliment someone can give you? (Even if it isn't true, you would like to hear it!)
6. If you knew you couldn't fail, what would you change in your life?
7. Are you fun to live with? Why or why not?
8. What is your personal definition of success?
9. Are you a success by your own definition? Yes or no?
10. What do you feel is the main motivator in your life? (What keeps you going?)
11. Complete this sentence: "I feel most important when . . ."
12. Do you feel you have any personal power in your life? Yes or no?
13. What has happened in the last seven days to cause you to answer yes or no?
14. What is the greatest problem or challenge you are currently facing in either your personal or professional life?
15. Describe briefly where you are in life. (Bored, excited; challenged, lost; at a crossroads, drifting, and so on.)
16. How did you get there?

INTERPRETATION OF VALUES INVENTORY

1. Compare your answers to questions 1 and 8. What you want most out of life and your definition of success should be fairly compatible.

2. Look at your answer to #4. Most people find it difficult to think good things about themselves, let alone write them down. When you have finished working through this book, it is hoped that you will be able to list a *lot* of things you like about yourself.

3. Consider your response to question 5. The finest compliment you could possibly receive is possibly your highest sense of value. We are motivated by our values; that is, what is important to us.

4. Compare your answers to questions 5 and 10. In 10, the question of what you think motivates you was direct. How similar are your replies to 5 and 10? If they are not similar, is it possible that 5 is a greater motivator in your life than 10?

5. Consider question 6. If people were without fear and knew that they could not fail, the three most common things they would change, in order, would be:
   a. A relationship (getting into or out of one)
   b. Their vocation
   c. Where they live

6. Examine your reply to question 7. About two-thirds of the people tested believe they are fun to live with. The most common general reason for being fun to live with is a sense of humor. People who are not fun to live with know why. This means they could be fun if they chose to be. Some people indicate they would be fun to live with if they were living with the right person. This, of course, is to avoid the issue.

7. Look at your reply to question 8. What we are looking for here is whether you define success in terms of "being" or "doing."

8. In response to question 9, nearly 50 percent of the people tested indicate they are not successful by their own definitions. Their idea is, I will *be* as soon as I *do.*

9. Look at your response to question 10. If all motivation can be reduced to a common denominator of love or fear, try to determine what your "bottom line" motivator is.

10. The most common answers to item 11 are, in order:
    a. When I am *doing* something
    b. When I *know* something
    c. When I am *with* someone special
11. In answer to question 12, 95 percent of people tested believe they have power. Of the 5 percent who believe they have *no* power, most score fairly low on the self-esteem analysis. They feel like "victims."
12. Examine your response to question 13. How we *use* power is the major determining factor in deciding whether we are "good" people or "bad" people.
13. Replying to question 14, the number one problem people face in every one of our seminars has been relationships.
14. The significance of questions 16 and 17 is to help us see that wherever we say we are in life, we are there by *choice*. The most frequent answer to 17 is "hard work." This is somewhat related to the frequent definition of success (question 8) in terms of *doing*.

INSTRUCTIONS FOR TAKING SELF-ESTEEM EXERCISE

This self-esteem exercise is designed to help you put your feelings about yourself into perspective. There are fifty statements on the exercise. The thing to keep in mind is: How *true* are the statements in relationship to you: Always, Usually, Occasionally, Rarely, or Never? Circle the number (4, 3, 2, 1, 0) that most closely represents your feelings *at this time*. Total the numbers in each column and add them together for a final score. Use the form on page 179 for your scoring.

SELF-ESTEEM EXERCISE

4 = Always; 3 = Usually; 2 = Occasionally;
1 = Rarely; 0 = Never

1. If I were a member of the opposite sex, I would find me attractive.
2. I feel well dressed.
3. I enjoy being seen in a bathing suit.
4. I like being seen at parties and other social occasions.
5. My weight is close to where I want it.
6. I like looking at myself in a full-length mirror.
7. I enjoy shopping for new clothes.
8. If someone hurts my feelings, I tell them.
9. I see the bright side of most situations.
10. I feel important as a person.
11. I can handle my own in a conversation.
12. People *value* my ideas and opinions.
13. I am not easily discouraged.
14. I am in a good mood.
15. I am energetic.
16. I feel good about my sexuality.
17. I can laugh at my own mistakes.
18. I feel intelligent.

19. I deserve the very best. Nothing is too good for me.
20. I easily forgive; I don't bear grudges.
21. I like me as I am.
22. I feel I am in control of my future.
23. I can do almost anything I really set my mind to.
24. Other people like me.
25. I enjoy meeting and talking to new people.
26. I accept responsibility for everything I think, feel, say, and do.
27. I feel good about other people's good fortune.
28. There's very little I am ashamed of.
29. If I had my life to live over, I wouldn't change much.
30. My life has been very interesting.
31. I feel I have accomplished something important in life.
32. I like the place where I live.
33. I enjoy my vocation.
34. I am able to confide in people.
35. I do not find fault with my family, friends, or associates.
36. People generally admire me.
37. I am open and honest and not afraid of letting people see my real self.
38. I am still growing as a person.
39. I am friendly, thoughtful, and generous toward others.
40. I am a kind person.
41. Luck plays only a *small* part in my life.
42. I enjoy getting up in the morning.
43. I would be *difficult* to replace.
44. My life is full.
45. I can take care of myself.
46. Other people need me.
47. I have done very little that worries me.
48. I am able to graciously accept compliments and gifts.
49. I've got a style that is unmistakably my own.
50. If I ever got in trouble, my friends would be right there, helping.

SCORING SHEET FOR SELF-ESTEEM EXERCISE

	Always	Usually	Occa-sionally	Rarely	Never
1.	4	3	2	1	0
2.	4	3	2	1	0
3.	4	3	2	1	0
4.	4	3	2	1	0
5.	4	3	2	1	0
6.	4	3	2	1	0
7.	4	3	2	1	0
8.	4	3	2	1	0
9.	4	3	2	1	0
10.	4	3	2	1	0
11.	4	3	2	1	0
12.	4	3	2	1	0
13.	4	3	2	1	0
14.	4	3	2	1	0
15.	4	3	2	1	0
16.	4	3	2	1	0
17.	4	3	2	1	0
18.	4	3	2	1	0
19.	4	3	2	1	0
20.	4	3	2	1	0
21.	4	3	2	1	0
22.	4	3	2	1	0
23.	4	3	2	1	0
24.	4	3	2	1	0
25.	4	3	2	1	0
Sub-Total	—	—	—	—	—

	Always	Usually	Occa-sionally	Rarely	Never
26.	4	3	2	1	0
27.	4	3	2	1	0
28.	4	3	2	1	0
29.	4	3	2	1	0
30.	4	3	2	1	0
31.	4	3	2	1	0
32.	4	3	2	1	0
33.	4	3	2	1	0
34.	4	3	2	1	0
35.	4	3	2	1	0
36.	4	3	2	1	0
37.	4	3	2	1	0
38.	4	3	2	1	0
39.	4	3	2	1	0
40.	4	3	2	1	0
41.	4	3	2	1	0
42.	4	3	2	1	0
43.	4	3	2	1	0
44.	4	3	2	1	0
45.	4	3	2	1	0
46.	4	3	2	1	0
47.	4	3	2	1	0
48.	4	3	2	1	0
49.	4	3	2	1	0
50.	4	3	2	1	0
Total Score	—	—	—	—	—

INTERPRETATION OF
SELF-ESTEEM EXERCISE

The total possible score on this exercise is 200. If you scored above 180, there is the possibility you were exaggerating. To score this high, you obviously must circle a lot of 4's. A 4 means *always* and always is an absolute; there are no exceptions. A person with a very high score may have a tendency to be rigid and slightly out of touch with reality. Perhaps the attitude is, "That is the way it *should* be, and I can't bear to admit there are moments when it isn't."

If you scored below 100, you were probably exaggerating also. It indicates that you have a habit of anticipating the worst—and then fulfilling your own expectations.

In each class that we give this exercise, we look for the curve. An average of 60 percent will score *between* 130 and 159. More often than not, more people will score *below 130* than those who score *above 160*.

GROWTH INHIBITORS

... When our fear of being rejected, or fear of being close, or of sharing our feelings with another person, inhibits interpersonal relationships.

... When the need for detail and information or the need to control becomes excessive and interferes with relationships.

... When we distort or exaggerate—either positively or negatively—a given area of life and fail to give an honest or realistic picture.

... When we fail to identify the fears in ourselves, hence, take no action to deal with these fears in a loving manner.

... When we refuse to do the loving thing—toward ourselves or in relation to others.

... When we permit the thoughts, feelings, behaviors, or expectations of others to become ours without first having thought them through for ourselves.

... When we permit our needs to become overwhelming in an interpersonal relationship or situation, and therefore, trigger fear responses in the other person.

... When we consistently trigger fear in the other person in an interpersonal relationship or situation.

... When we stay in positions, occupations, or professional or personal relationships in which our needs are neither met nor likely to be met.

... When we are unaware of what our needs happen to be, hence, permit our feelings to lead us in interpersonal relationships that are not likely to be satisfying or long-lasting.

... When we utilize our actions and/or behaviors in the attempt to prove that we are somebody or that we are a certain kind of person.

... When we fail to act to meet our needs.

... When we ignore what our feelings are telling us.

... When we fail to set goals in life.

... When we think that our personal security lies outside ourselves.

... When we purchase things we do not need simply because they are presented as bargains.

... When we dehumanize people by calling them names or pinning labels on them.

... When we allow unhealthy input to enter our minds.

... When we surrender the control and responsibility for our happiness to someone or something outside ourselves.

... When we make comparisons.

... When we fear people because we have surrendered our personal power (responsibility).

... When we blame someone or something outside ourselves for our being wherever we happen to be in life.

... When we fail to utilize our personal resources to make our lives more productive, exciting, and purposeful.

... When we give "you" messages.

... When the focus of our lives is on the past or the future to such an extent that we are immobilized in the present.

CHECKPOINTS FOR GROWTH

You can use this graph to check your growth process.

Place an *x* where you feel you were when you started the book.

Place a *y* where you feel you were when you finished the book.

Example 1 ⌊⌋⌊⌋⌊x⌋⌊⌋⌊y⌋⌊⌋⌊⌋⌊⌋ 15

1. I am more interesting 1 ⌊⌋⌊⌋⌊⌋⌊⌋⌊⌋⌊⌋⌊⌋⌊⌋ 15

2. It is easier for me to listen to those who disagree with me. ⌊⌋⌊⌋⌊⌋⌊⌋⌊⌋⌊⌋⌊⌋⌊⌋

3. I feel a strong sense of my self-worth. ⌊⌋⌊⌋⌊⌋⌊⌋⌊⌋⌊⌋⌊⌋⌊⌋

4. I feel I trust my own insights. ⌊⌋⌊⌋⌊⌋⌊⌋⌊⌋⌊⌋⌊⌋⌊⌋

5. I am not afraid of what someone might think. ⌊⌋⌊⌋⌊⌋⌊⌋⌊⌋⌊⌋⌊⌋⌊⌋

6. I have a good sense of humor. ⌊⌋⌊⌋⌊⌋⌊⌋⌊⌋⌊⌋⌊⌋⌊⌋

7. I am interested in lots of things. ⌊⌋⌊⌋⌊⌋⌊⌋⌊⌋⌊⌋⌊⌋⌊⌋

8. I feel I have a lot of courage. ⌊⌋⌊⌋⌊⌋⌊⌋⌊⌋⌊⌋⌊⌋⌊⌋

9. I am genuinely interested in others. ⌊⌋⌊⌋⌊⌋⌊⌋⌊⌋⌊⌋⌊⌋⌊⌋

10. I give more time to others—ungrudgingly. ⌊⌋⌊⌋⌊⌋⌊⌋⌊⌋⌊⌋⌊⌋⌊⌋

11. I am not afraid to be "needy." ⌊⌋⌊⌋⌊⌋⌊⌋⌊⌋⌊⌋⌊⌋⌊⌋

12. I am more generous with my means. ⌊⌋⌊⌋⌊⌋⌊⌋⌊⌋⌊⌋⌊⌋⌊⌋

13. It is easy for me to feel the joy and pain of others. ⌊⌋⌊⌋⌊⌋⌊⌋⌊⌋⌊⌋⌊⌋⌊⌋

14. I feel deserving of the good things in life. ⌊⌋⌊⌋⌊⌋⌊⌋⌊⌋⌊⌋⌊⌋⌊⌋

15. Other _____

    _____ ⌊⌋⌊⌋⌊⌋⌊⌋⌊⌋⌊⌋⌊⌋⌊⌋

THE GREAT LOVER'S MANIFESTO

Love is a decision; a commitment; a covenant.

Love is given with no thought of return.

Love wills to act in the other's highest interest.

Love accepts because it loves; not because of something on the part of the other.

Love acknowledges and is sensitive to the needs of the one loved.

Love is not a feeling; but a relationship needs warm and loving feelings to support the intentions of my love.

Love is a commitment forever; a permanent thing; a life-wager— not as long as, or until anything.

Love forgives and forgets the failings of the one loved.

Love lets me begin again without handicap.

Love is unceasing, unearned, integrating, and personal.

Love is the surrender of a certain portion of my sovereignty.

Love means the unreserved giving of myself for the benefit of the other, even if it cost me my life.

Love is liberating.

Love cannot be banked.

Love is never on stage.

Love is a lover of truth—even about myself.

Love and authenticity are inseparable partners.

Love comes in and defenses drop, freedom begins and fatigue moves out.

Love esteems and affirms the unique value of the one loved.

Love's submissive authority wins because it doesn't fear losing.

Love is the non-possessive delight in the particularity of the other.

Love's irony is that when I need it the most I am the most unlovely.

Love is costly, but the alternatives are deadly.

The most loving thing I will ever do will probably be the hardest.

I need to know the love you offer me is a permanent offer before I will give up my security operations, my masks, roles, and games.

Love exists when the satisfaction, security, and development of the other person becomes as significant to me as my own satisfaction, security, and development.

When I am no longer afraid of neediness, I am no longer afraid of love.

If I have love in my life, it can make up for a great many things I lack. If I do not have love, no matter what else there is, it is not enough.

The ultimate success of my life will not be judged by those who admire me for my accomplishments, but by the number of those who attribute their wholeness to my loving them, by the number of those who have seen their true beauty and worth in my eyes.

Bibliography

Ahlem, Lloyd H. *Do I Have to Be Me?* Ventura, Calif.: Regal Books, 1973.

Becker, Ernest. *The Denial of Death.* New York: Free Press, 1973.

Branden, Nathaniel. *Psychology of Self-Esteem.* New York: Bantam, 1971.

Briggs, Dorothy C. *Your Child's Self-Esteem: The Key to His Life.* Garden City, N.Y.: Doubleday, 1970.

Bristol, Claude. *The Magic of Believing.* New York: Pocket Books, 1967.

Broadbent, W.W. *How to Be Loved.* Englewood Cliffs, N.J.: Prentice-Hall, 1976.

Campbell, David P. *If You Don't Know Where You're Going, You'll Probably End up Somewhere Else.* Allen, Tex.: Argus Communications, 1974.

Clason, George S. *The Richest Man in Babylon.* New York: E.P. Dutton, 1955.

Chambers, Oswald. *My Utmost for His Highest.* New York: Dodd, Mead & Co., 1925.

Dobson, James. *Hide or Seek.* Old Tappan, N.J.: Revell, 1974.

Drummond, Henry. *The Greatest Thing in the World.* Old Tappan, N.J.: Revell, 1968.

Frankl, Viktor. *Man's Search for Meaning.* New York: Pocket Books, 1980.

Friedman, Martha. *Overcoming the Fear of Success.* New York: Seaview Books, 1980.

Gallwey, W. Timothy. *The Inner Game of Tennis.* New York: Random House, 1974.

Goble, Frank. *The Third Force.* New York: Grossman, 1970.

Goldberg, Herb, and Lewis, Robert T. *Money Madness.* New York: William Morrow & Co., 1978.

Grant, Dave. *Heavy Questions.* Ventura, Calif.: Regal Books, 1972.

Grant, Dave. *You've Got What It Takes.* Seattle: Rainbow Publications, 1973.

Harris, Thomas. *I'm OK—You're OK: A Practical Guide to Transactional Analysis.* New York: Harper & Row, 1967.

Hill, Napoleon. *Think and Grow Rich.* New York: Fawcett, 1979.

Hodges, Marshall Bryant. *Your Fear of Love.* Garden City, N.Y.: Doubleday, 1969.

Howe, Reuel L. *The Miracle of Dialogue.* New York: Seabury Press, 1980.

Koile, Earl. *Listening as a Way of Becoming.* Waco, Tex.: Word, 1977.

Lair, Jess. *I Ain't Much Baby—But I'm All I've Got.* New York: Fawcett, 1978.

Lembo, John. *Help Yourself.* Allen, Tex.: Argus Communications, 1974.

Maltz, Maxwell. *Psycho-Cybernetics: The New Way to a Successful Life.* Englewood Cliffs, N.J.: Prentice-Hall, 1960.

Mandino, Og. *The Greatest Salesman in the World.* New York: Fell, 1968.

Mandino, Og. *The Greatest Miracle in the World.* New York: Fell, 1975.

Marquis, Dave M. *Making Love a Way of Life.* Allen Tex.: Argus Communications, 1977.

Maslow, Abraham. *Motivation and Personality.* New York: Harper & Row, 1970.

Meilaender, Gilbert. *A Taste of the Other.* Grand Rapids, Mich.: William B. Eerdmans, 1978.

Menninger, Karl. *Whatever Became of Sin?* New York: Hawthorn Books, 1973.

Osborne, Cecil. *The Art of Understanding Yourself.* Grand Rapids, Mich.: Zondervan, 1967.

Peale, Norman Vincent. *Positive Imaging.* Old Tappan, N.J.: Revell, 1982.

Pearce, Joseph Chilton, *Magical Child.* New York: E.P. Dutton, 1977.

Ponder, Catherine. *The Dynamic Laws of Prosperity.* Englewood Cliffs, N.J.: Prentice-Hall, 1962.

Powell, John. *Why Am I Afraid to Tell You Who I Am?* Allen, Tex.: Argus Communications, 1969.

Powell, John. *Full Human Fully Alive.* Allen, Tex.: Argus Communications, 1974.

Powell, John. *The Secret of Staying in Love.* Allen, Tex.: Argus Communications, 1974.

Powell, John. *Unconditional Love.* Allen, Tex.: Argus Communications, 1978.

Rubin, Theodore. *The Angry Book.* New York: Macmillan, 1969.

Rubin, Theodore. *Compassion and Self-Hate.* New York: David McKay, 1975.

Simon, Sidney B. *Meeting Yourself Halfway.* Allen, Tex.: Argus Communications, 1974.

Tec, Leon. *The Fear of Success.* New York: NAL, 1978.

Viscott, David. *How to Live with Another Person.* New York: Arbor House, 1974.

Wagner, Maurice E. *The Sensation of Being Somebody.* Grand Rapids, Mich.: Zondervan, 1975.

For information regarding Dave Grant's

*Maximum Performer Seminars
*Audio Cassettes
*Video Cassettes
*Affirmation Card Sets
*Other Books
*Pendant for lapel or necklace to signify
your decision to become a Great Lover
*Parchment copy of The Great Lover's Manifesto
suitable for framing

Write to him at:

The Growth Process Institute
P.O. Box 273
Encino, CA 91316